FINANCIAL SAVVY FOR THERAPISTS

HOW TO MANAGE YOUR MONEY TO BUILD YOUR BUSINESS

ALEXA S. ELKINGTON

Financial Savvy for Therapists: How To Manage Your Money To Build Your Business

Copyright © 2016 by Alexa S. Elkington
Published by Savvy Money Books

Editorial Production: Janet Spencer King,
www.bookdevelopmentgroup.com
Cover Design: Lisa Hainline
Interior Design: Laurie Musick Wright, LMW Design, Inc.

All rights reserved. No part of this book may be reproduced, stored in a retrieval system, or transmitted in any form or by any means, electronic, mechanical, or otherwise, without the prior written permission of the publisher, except for brief quotations in articles and reviews.

Visit the author at www.savvymoneybooks.com

Printed in the United States of America for Worldwide Distribution

ISBN: 978-0-9972620-0-1

Advance Praise for
Financial Savvy for Therapists:
How to Manage Your Money
to Build Your Business

Alexa Elkington's "Financial Savvy for Therapists" achieves the impossible. This excellent book both informs *and* inspires therapists to become financially savvy by developing a business mindset. Alexa gives innovative, practical ways to think about money that clear the air about what she calls "cloud problems," that is financial issues that, like clouds, are changing, difficult to grasp, and unpredictable. Her insightful quizzes are illuminating and make it easy for you, the professional, to define and deal with your elusive financial challenges. We are proud to recommend this book. *Ellyn Bader, PhD and Peter Pearson, PhD, founders and directors of The Couples Institute®*

In this book Alexa Elkington perfectly lays out how to set up a therapy practice. Before becoming a successful therapist, she worked as an accountant giving her the knowledge that most therapists lack—and what they sorely need. How I wish I could have read this book before I started my practice some 40 years ago. I would have saved many hours—and false starts—by learning the importance of a business mindset and the implementation of solid financial principles. Read this book even if you are an experienced therapist now. You will learn how to tighten all your business procedures to make yourself financially protected. You will be working smarter, not harder. *Patricia A. White, PhD*

Alexa powerfully slays the notion that it's an oxymoron to put 'mental health professional' and 'business mindset' together. She weaves relevant examples from colleagues, clients, friends and family into her accounting experience to activate real-time tools. Even though I've been a successful businesswoman in the self-employed field for 35 years, the information I gained from reading her book makes me feel completely comfortable calling myself a 'Savvy Money Therapist.' *Judith Pinkerton, LPMT, MT-BC, founder/president of Music 4 Life® Center*

To say I was surprised by how much I enjoyed reading this book would be a complete understatement. Money expert and marriage and family therapist, Alexa Elkington, outlines the essential business principles every therapist should know, and she does it with elegance and simplicity, skillfully blending her business acumen with her therapeutic skills. We follow the journey of Becky, a psychotherapist who is fulfilling her dream of switching from agency work to private practice. But the stress she has from her lack of financial planning knowledge, her ineffective business practices, and her own personal blocks stand in her way. Fortunately Alexa shares an office with Becky and is there to advise her as she begins to feel overwhelmed. We all need an Alexa in our lives. *Nancy St. John, MIACP, Marriage and Relationship Counsellor*

Alexa uses a powerful mix of compassionate understanding of therapist's beliefs and essential business accounting practice to help us become financially astute business owners. She combines her years of experience as a therapist and, before that, an accountant to teach us all that we can take charge of our finances ... An important read for both new and experienced therapists–all therapists. *Paula E. Dennan, Registered Clinical Psychologist, Director STNZ*

DEDICATION

When the student is ready, the teacher will appear.

I dedicate this book to the many "teachers" in my life who appeared at the exact time I was ready and hungry for their direction, their coaching, and their encouragement. Some of you know the role you have performed in my life; others may not be aware of the impact you've had on me. I have learned from many.

Thank you all.

Acknowledgments

In the preface that follows, I write about the crucial role Ellyn Bader, PhD, and Peter Pearson, PhD, played in making this book a reality. I gratefully acknowledge both of them as well as my gratitude for their commitment to teaching and to leading therapists who desire to become better clinicians and more successful in business.

It was while I was taking part in Ellyn and Peter's Master Mentorship Group that I conceived the idea for this book. As our year together progressed, their continued encouragement kept me moving forward. I also greatly appreciate the enthusiasm and feedback that the eleven other members of the mentor group offered me during the sometimes agonizing times I experienced while writing this book.

Had it not been for my amazing editor, Janet Spencer King, I would never have gotten past "go." In the planning stages, Janet helped me organize my thoughts and ideas as I struggled with how to present the concepts in a clear, understandable way that didn't make me sound like an accountant. When you read this book, I believe you will see that she did indeed succeed in helping me make the book entertaining as well as informative.

Because of my Monday-through-Friday therapy business schedule, I spent much of my weekends writing. I want to acknowledge the patience and supportiveness my spouse exhibited as weekend after weekend, I secluded myself in my office. An evening out was a rare event during this venture, and I thank you for your support and encouragement.

Contents

Preface 9
Introduction 13
Part 1: Cloud Problems 17
1. The First Cloud: Personal Money Attitudes and Beliefs 19
2. Business "Think": A Business Mind-Set 29
3. Mental Health Care: Bottom of the Totem Pole 37
Part 2: Clock Issues 43
4. Setting the Stage for Your Business Numbers 45
5. Private Practice: Things You Need to Know 47
6. Things That Make Your Life Easier 65
7. And Finally, The One Thing You'll Be Really Glad You Did ... 71
8. Introducing the Numbers: A Brief Interlude Before We Meet Them 75
9. It Costs How Much?: Overhead 79
10. Meet Your Income Statement 89
11. How Much Do I Get to Keep?: Profit-Margin Ratio 99
12. Just Enough: The Break-Even Point 103
13. Check Your Gas Gauge: Cash Flow 109
14. Staying on Track: Bank Reconciliation 115
15. Struggles with Fees: Setting the Right Fee 119
16. Be Prepared: Tax Wisdom 127
17. What Is Your Business Worth?: Meet Your Balance Sheet ... 133
18. Setting a Schedule: What to Do When 141
About the Author 151
Appendix 153

Preface

Why financial savvy…for mental health care professionals?

For many therapists, this work is truly a calling. The pleasure of meeting new clients and helping them understand where they're coming from and how to find a better road ahead gives practitioners a great deal of satisfaction. In spite of that, there are many therapists who are settling for less—less money, less success, less opportunity, less work, less recognition, less time, and less pleasure in doing what they love.

Some therapists opt for agency work, trading off long hours and heavy caseloads for a set salary, health benefits, and maybe a pension plan. Others work in private practice with full schedules and many clients, and there are also those who work privately but put in fewer hours, considering therapy a "side" job. Regardless of their particular places, the therapists I've met have often expressed frustration and the feeling of being stuck in their current situations. Why, then, do they not change that?

The dream of establishing a private practice that provides security and financial success as well as professional satisfaction is common among mental health professionals. But achieving it remains a major challenge for many. The reason, as I have observed again and again, is that for the most part, practitioners have little or no financial savvy. Few of them have had an opportunity to learn the basic financial principles that form the foundation of a sound business.

The purpose of this book is to change that. In the pages that follow, you'll learn the specific information you need to turn your therapy *practice* into a therapy *business*. You will develop the *business mind-set* that will get you there. I will explain in detail what you need to do on a daily, weekly, monthly, and yearly basis—and why. In my mind, I see trying to run a business without these basic accounting principles as a bit like parking your car at Disneyland without any designated parking spots. Haphazard parking—parking wherever and whenever you want—would produce chaos just as surely as running a business without a sound financial structure would. When you learn about business and money, though, you'll know, metaphorically speaking, where your car is parked so that you can find it quickly and move smoothly through the parking lot and onto the highway of possibilities.

You may be wondering how it came to be that I could write a book for mental health care professionals that explains what they need to know about money. *What does she know, and why did she write this book?* Fair enough.

I am a licensed marriage and family therapist in Las Vegas, Nevada. For more than twenty years, I have run my own private therapy business; my business partner and I also rent office space to a group of licensed clinicians. Before I became a therapist, I worked in accounting and tax firms. I was fortunate to work with a gentleman who valued my ability to work with clients as well as with the numbers required to prepare financial statements and tax returns. At his encouragement, I took the IRS Special Enrollment Examination, and on completion of it, I received an official tax preparer's license and earned the legal right to represent a client in a tax audit.

The majority of the accounting firm's clients were medical professionals. As part of the services we provided to them, we met in their offices on a monthly or quarterly basis to review their latest financial statements and to discuss their financial challenges and the ways they could increase their business and productivity. I observed the wide range of income, both gross income and net, that these professionals brought in, and it fascinated me. The dramatic difference in their earnings told me that there was much more to building a successful business as a service provider than just becoming a licensed professional.

When I left that profession to fulfill my dream of becoming a psychotherapist, I naturally applied the financial principles I had learned to my own business. My practice grew, we survived the recession, and time moved on.

Late in 2014 I read that Ellyn Bader, PhD, and Peter Pearson, PhD, of the Couples Institute were offering a one-year mentorship program for therapists who wanted to transcend to a new level of doing/being. I was familiar with the couple after seeing them present at seminars and studying for over a year in their online couples-therapy training program. I took a big breath, applied for the mentorship program, and was accepted.

Our group of twelve professionals from all over the world first met in January 2015. Sitting with therapists who'd come together to overcome personal blocks and to transform their professional lives was like nothing I'd ever experienced before. It was energizing, collaborative, and supportive. Ideas that might have felt impossible to even consider became sustainable realities in that group. Without it, I would have never had even a glimmer of a thought about writing a book. It was in that space—a space where possibilities were alive and honored—that this book was conceived.

We have all heard and maybe even spoken the money narrative that most therapists share: "I'm just not good with money. Who wants to do that boring stuff? Why bother?" I see that narrative as a huge roadblock for any professional who wants to build a sustainable business. It is time to put that thinking aside, to learn financial basics, to apply the procedures, and to build the business therapists want and deserve. Be the professional you are. Let this book provide you with the information and the inspiration you need to guide you through this transition.

This is why *Financial Savvy for Therapists.*

INTRODUCTION

For Rent: Professional office space available for mental health care professional. Are you thinking about starting or expanding your own private practice? We are a group of eight professionals—psychologists, MFTs, and MSWs—looking for just the right licensed mental health care professional to occupy our last available office. Our office is located in a desirable area of the city. All the usual office amenities included.

As I finished writing the ad, I smiled in satisfaction and pushed "send." It was then on its way to be displayed on websites for mental health professionals. My hopes were high that just the right individual would show up to rent our last remaining empty office, which had recently been vacated by Becky, a psychotherapist who had come to us about nine years prior.

Becky had previously worked for a state-run agency. Thanks to the experience and supervision she had received there, she'd felt ready to leave that nest and to pursue her dream of having her own practice. Her clinical skills seemed solidly in place. She was enthusiastic and had a pleasant way about her that we were sure would help clients feel comfortable and cared for. Our impressions of her were all positive—she would be a wonderful addition to our office.

Becky told me that she felt confident about being able to run her own business. She didn't see the change as any cause for concern. People would come to her, schedule their next appointment, and pay her, and that would be that. And oh yes, she knew her rent would be due at the beginning of each month, but she was certain that her appointment book would fill up quickly and that she would always pay it on time.

About three months after Becky started, I noticed that she wasn't quite as cheerful or as optimistic as she had been when she'd first arrived. One afternoon when the office was quiet, I invited her into my office to chat about how her practice was coming along. I explained that I just wanted to check in with her and give her a chance to share any concerns she might have had. She hesitated for a moment but then took me up on my offer.

Within moments, Becky's fears and concerns began to spill out. She worried about not having enough clients, about not having enough money, and about whether the fee she charged was appropriate. Becky added that she didn't know how to keep track of the money she did get or how to keep track of whether a client still owed her money. Her worries didn't stop there. Added to her list were concerns about collecting overdue fees from clients and handling insurance companies—and what about estimated tax forms for the government?

Close to tears, Becky confided in me that her anxiety about money was leading to sleepless nights. In fact, she said, she felt like she was a mess and perhaps didn't belong in private practice after all.

As I listened to Becky's anguish, I thought of my own experiences of building my private practice. Of course, I'd had the usual challenges—establishing my name, developing marketing strategies, and building a clientele—but I was fortunate that my background had provided me with

INTRODUCTION

a skill many mental health professionals lack. For a number of years, I had worked in the accounting and tax field, which had given me expertise concerning financial issues and how to handle them. I wanted to help Becky learn the skills she needed to handle money and the financial issues involved in running a successful business.

We discussed the all-too-true axiom that when it comes to money, like so many things in life, if we don't manage it, it will manage us. I assured Becky that I would be glad to teach her the fundamentals of good financial management, specifically as they apply to running a private practice. We agreed to meet several times a week to discuss matters of money, including the stumbling blocks unique to a private practice and how to overcome them. Becky needed an action plan to get her going. Once she developed financial savvy, I was sure that she would take control of her business and that her confidence level would soar.

Part of her action plan was to have a goal. Becky looked forward to the feeling she would have once she'd completed her financial education and implemented what she'd learned. To help her gain a sense of what that would be, I gave her this visualization to practice:

As you put your head down on your pillow each night, you are calm and relaxed. Financial worries are in the past. Your finances are well organized, your appointment calendar is full, your clients pay on time, and you are meeting your bills. You are free of money intruders running around inside your head as you close your eyes and drift restfully into sleep.

Part 1:
Cloud Problems

1

THE FIRST CLOUD: PERSONAL MONEY ATTITUDES AND BELIEFS

I gave a lot of thought as to what topic could best begin Becky's financial education. As a therapist and a former accountant, I'm able to see both sides of the money perspective in a double view that sheds light on two different sets of problems. I categorize them as "cloud" problems and "clock" problems.

Ultimately, I determined that cloud problems were clearly the place to start. Like clouds, these types of money problems are undefined, always changing, difficult to grasp, and unpredictable. Few people understand cloud problems for the simple reason that many, perhaps most, people are unaware of their relationship to money, including their prejudices about money as well as their beliefs, fears, expectations, and financial habits. A lack of such an awareness subjects people to cloud problems that can transform what could be a bright, comfortable experience into a torrential internal storm. In those cases, money difficulties can feel like a tornado ripping through one's life and leaving behind feelings of helplessness and hopelessness.

The cloud issues that are crucial to confront and explore are many. All involve personal core beliefs about money.

Some of these issues include the following:
- general attitudes toward money
- how we make it
- how we spend it
- how we save it or don't save it
- how we view and feel about people who make a lot of money
- how we view and feel about people who have little money
- how we view our own worthiness to have money
- what "shame" issues we hold on to about money.

Cloud issues are major stumbling blocks in general, but for people who are self-employed and seek to create some level of financial security, cloud problems become even more intense because in the case of the self-employed, they involve self-worth, ego, and self-esteem. The self-employed tend to translate a business failure into a personal failure rather than a bad business venture. Personalizing what is in fact business turns it into a heavier responsibility rife with potential danger and pitfalls.

Yes, this was exactly where Becky and I needed to begin. As you will discover, Becky's cloud was filled with destructive beliefs about money.

Exploring Money Beliefs: What, Where, and How

I started by having Becky write out her beliefs about money. The areas she was to explore were quite specific and would lead to the foundation she had created for her every-

The First Cloud: Personal Money Attitudes and Beliefs

day money behaviors. I asked her the following questions about money:

- What did you learn about money from your family?
- Do feelings of guilt or shame lurk in your money beliefs? What are they?
- What would it be like if you made more money than your father ever did or more money than your spouse?
- What are the core money beliefs you hold on to?
- What beliefs do you have that fill you with fear and insecurity?
- What are your feelings about being compensated for the services you provide clients?
- What beliefs do you have that help you build a thriving, financially successful business?

Becky brought her "money beliefs" file with her to our next meeting. She had expected the exercise to take around ten minutes at the most. Much to her surprise, she had spent hours recalling episodes in her past that involved money and finances. As she wrote about and pondered her money beliefs, it became clear to her how her experiences had shaped many of her money beliefs and her feelings of being worthy of having money.

The first area Becky tackled had to do with her parents' attitudes and habits regarding money—and how she'd absorbed many of their beliefs and fears. She recalled hearing the fights that had taken place between her parents regarding the prioritization of how family money was spent. Her parents were from different value systems, and that resulted in tension concerning both spending and saving. While Becky was too young to know much of anything about money, she knew it must be important, since her parents so often became loud and upset when discussing the subject. In her young mind, she decided she would never get attached to money; she felt that that way, she would never respond to it in the ways she saw around her.

Negative Money Beliefs

Becky's thorough exploration of her beliefs and our discussion provided insight and clarification that enabled her to describe her relationship with money. Once we reviewed and discussed her money beliefs, we looked at the impact they had on her behavior. Whether closely held beliefs are known or unknown, they impact almost all behaviors, and Becky was no exception.

Then I had Becky create a chart in which she outlined her negative beliefs and the behaviors that resulted from each of them. On the left side of the sheet, Becky listed the negative beliefs that she had about money. On the right side of the sheet, she named the actions that were the result of her negative beliefs.

Negative Beliefs I hold about Money	Behaviors That Result from Those Beliefs

One of Becky's key beliefs was that she couldn't be the "successful one" in her family. The reason was simple: everyone considered her older brother to be the bright, charming "winner." As a child, Becky had felt that it would be acceptable for her to do okay, but she hadn't felt that she should expect to rise above that. The superstar position in the family had already been filled. Thus, Becky's expectation that

THE FIRST CLOUD: PERSONAL MONEY ATTITUDES AND BELIEFS

she would never be anything more than "mildly" successful had taken hold.

When Becky traced the behavior that resulted from that belief, she could see the many ways she sabotaged her own success. She admitted that she often failed to return phone calls that had come in from potential clients, instead telling herself she would get to them later. Underlying her behavior was the fear that she would not be able to answer the callers' questions sufficiently and that, consequently, they would not schedule an appointment with her. By avoiding the calls, she was able to avoid the possibility of being rejected by potential clients.

Becky also revealed that she hadn't developed a plan about how she would move forward toward her goals. In fact, she admitted that the only time she had set goals was in grad school. She had mostly taken a more passive attitude toward her life, figuring that if something was meant to be, it would come her way. Not surprisingly, she'd ended up with no apparent organization as well as a tendency to procrastinate in her personal and business life. Becky explained that thinking about goals and structure made her feel overwhelmed and like she had no idea of where to begin.

Becky's go-to position was using mindless activities to avoid important tasks. That cycle left her feeling paralyzed, and that, in turn, fed her procrastination.

That paralysis led to stacks of unfinished work, unreturned phone calls, unpaid bills, and a struggling business. Nothing positive or enlightening could possibly come from her pattern of procrastination and disorganization. Becky could see how her poor habits had become a major source of energy depletion and could see the impact they'd had on meaningful accomplishments. It was time for her to make significant changes in her life. That, she recognized, was the only way she would become a successful private practitioner.

Positive Money Beliefs

It was then time for us to explore what Becky could do to change her destructive patterns. The goal was to replace them with positive beliefs that would create the potential for positive behaviors. The first step in this process was for Becky to describe her positive beliefs about money, including beliefs about having enough of it and even having more than enough. The last idea was a stretch for her—more than enough money! She wondered how that could possibly happen to her.

Becky attached many of her positive ideas to the ideas of being able to provide for herself and being able to contribute toward providing for her family. She added that she also wanted to be planning and saving for her future. Accomplishing those goals would allow Becky to experience the satisfying sense of being a good steward of the money she did have. The possibility that her bank statement would show that she had enough money to pay her bills with some left over delighted her. But she explained that at that point, she didn't have a clue about how to organize her finances. I was able to assure her that those issues were "clock" problems that we would get to as soon as we were ready to get out of the clouds.

An important aspect to creating a positive relationship with money for Becky, and indeed for all psychotherapists, is developing a greater appreciation of the value of one's work. In Becky's previous job at the agency, most of her

The First Cloud: Personal Money Attitudes and Beliefs

clients had been court ordered to attend therapy. In private practice, she was seeing people who had voluntarily made the decision to seek therapy. Those clients had come to therapy with the expectation that help was available. The therapist's skills, knowledge, and abilities to relate to others, to respond appropriately, and to give undivided attention to others come together to provide a positive and helpful experience for the client. In exchange for the therapist's time and expertise, the client assumes the responsibility of paying for the services, a fair exchange of energy.

Impact of Positive Money Beliefs

To track Becky's current positive beliefs as well as the positive beliefs she wanted to embrace as her own, we created a second chart. We then expanded it to include positive behaviors that coordinated with each positive belief.

Positive Beliefs I hold about Money	Behaviors That Result from Those Beliefs

I challenged Becky to review her positive money beliefs frequently and to immediately begin implementing the matching behaviors. One of the first alterations she made reflected her changed attitude and the higher value she placed on every person who made a phone call to her office. The natural behavioral follow-up, then, was to return each one of these calls in a timely fashion. Interestingly, another positive belief she developed directly concerned a financial institution: the bank. She learned to appreciate that the bank considered her worthy enough to loan money to and was comfortable that she would repay it as agreed. That enabled Becky to view the monthly act of paying her bill as a privilege rather than a drudgery.

Becky was excited and enthused about her first money lessons. Within just a few days, she began to map out and implement a growing list of specific behaviors.

Exploring Your Core Money Beliefs

Exploring the questions here along with the actions that follow them will help you recognize and understand your core money beliefs. Rather than responding to the quiz in your head, take the time and make the effort to write down your responses. Once you have completed your list, study it carefully. In doing so, you will see how your beliefs help—or hinder—your ability to make and handle money as a mental health professional in private practice.

Your Relationship with Money

- What are your core beliefs about money? (E.g., "My family has always been bad with money," "I just don't have what it takes to make a lot of money," "I would become snooty if I had money," "I'm not smart enough to make much money," "Other people just have it easier and are able to make money," or, "I spend money faster than I get it.")
- What does your overall picture show? Is it more positive than negative?
- Explore your attitude about money. Is it based on fear and a lack of money or on an abundance of money?

The First Cloud: Personal Money Attitudes and Beliefs

- Do you have confidence that an abundance of money exists and that you can make plenty of money in this profession?

Your Money Belief Chart

- Using the previous questions that Becky explored, make a chart that lists your positive and negative beliefs about money.
- List the corresponding negative and positive behaviors that you have formed as a result of your money beliefs. (There may be many of them.)
- Pay special attention to the beliefs that are blocking your success.
- Challenge yourself to go deep in your exploration of your money belief system and its impact on your behavior.

For a further exploration of this topic, go online and take our self-assessment at
www.savvymoneybooks.com.

2

BUSINESS "THINK": A BUSINESS MIND-SET

While writing this next chapter, I began to wonder if using the phrases "mental health professional" and "have a business mind-set" in the same sentence might hint of an oxymoron. Many times I've heard my fellow mental health care professionals say how much they dislike the business or money part of managing their practices. They describe their dislike for it with such comments as, "I'm just not good with money," and, "I get so uncomfortable talking about money with my clients—I don't like the money part."

They are very smart people, which led me to ponder why, exactly, business and finances are challenging for them.

As psychotherapists, we are completely comfortable exploring the inner workings of our clients' minds, and we do it for hours on a regular basis. We are well trained in working with the psyche and in discussing relationships, emotions, traumas, and the many other psychological issues that show up in our offices. The therapy work we do constantly activates the right side of the brain. But what about the left side of the brain? What is happening with it? As you're reading, learning, and applying this financial information, consider that you're providing your left brain some much-needed exercise.

Working in a private practice adds the description of "business owner" to one's professional status. Just as we know and understand the language of psychology, it behooves us to know and understand the language of business. There's no reason to panic or to rush to hide behind anxiety about money. The language of business involves basic business concepts that are not that complicated. You'll find that my descriptions of them are clear and easy to understand. There are no tornado clouds here.

What Is a "Business Mind-Set"?

Many of you may be in a situation similar to Becky's—that is, new to private practice, which means new to owning and operating a business. You probably have many questions about owning a business, starting with, "What *is* a business mind-set anyway, and what does it have to do with me? How do business owners think differently than I do?" Some of those differences may appear to be subtle, while others may be so bold that you can't miss them. Once you understand the concept of a business mind-set and expand your thinking to include one, you'll be able to create opportunities to grow your business. Indeed, you would be hard-pressed to find a successful business that doesn't incorporate these basic concepts into their overall strategy and daily functions.

Have an Objective

The first concept is simple but will likely require some

consideration: What is your objective for being in business? All business-minded thinkers have a clear objective. Usually the objective is to provide a service or a product that clients or customers will want to purchase, thereby creating an income flow for the business. As a clinician, you're constantly working to improve the service you provide. You read, attend lectures, and pursue more training to fulfill your objective of being a better clinician. Even with all your expertise, if you're not able to attract paying clients, you won't be able to fulfill your desire to have a successful business. As a business owner, your business objective must be to create an income flow, to increase the income flow, and to best manage the income you do earn. "How does every business decision I make affect the income in my business?" is a question that the business-minded person must consider. In both the start-up and the daily functioning of the business, each decision must be carefully evaluated through the filter of the objective to create and build income.

Let's use an example here to demonstrate how this principle works. Therapist Sally decides it's time to purchase a new couch for her office. She's tempted to rationalize buying one that costs much more money than is necessary because she has her eye on an expensive couch. She tells herself that since a couch is such an important item in her office, she really should purchase one of the highest quality. It would last so much longer. But when Sally runs this couch decision through her business mind-set, she asks herself the following question: how will this new couch help increase my revenue? *The business mind-set requires a direct positive correlation between expenditure and profit.*

If she sharpens up her office with a new couch, her clients will be more comfortable and will possibly perceive her as a more successful clinician. Maybe their increased comfort in her office will make them more willing to book further appointments. There's potentially a positive correlation here between the couch expenditure and a possible increase in profits.

But the idea that she *needs* an expensive couch is a rationalization that could lead her, like it could lead many of us, to make a decision that's not in the best interest of the business objective, which is, of course, to increase profits. It's crucial to know the difference between luxuries and necessities to prevent rationalizations that lead to bad decisions. The business mind knows that rationalization is the enemy of success.

Know Your Numbers

As mental health clinicians, we measure and observe our clients' behaviors, patterns, and progress (or possible regression). We are attuned to any changes our clients may display.

Being a business owner and taking good care of one's business involves the same type of responsibility. The methodology of taking care of a business is different, but it's equally important. Just as therapy has its own language, there's a specific vocabulary that's used in the business world. The vocabulary centers on certain numbers that represent the health of the business. The numbers and their organization provide valuable information to the business owner.

Starting with the basic numbers, the business-minded owner must keep a good eye on **revenue** and **expenses**. Monthly or quarterly financial statements referred to as **"income statements"** report these numbers. Another important set of numbers forms the **"cash-flow statement,"** which tracks the cash the business generates and uses in a specific time period. This statement helps business owners track the amount of cash in their accounts and understand how much cash will be needed in the near future. These two statements may look similar, but they provide very different information to you, the business owner, which we will discuss in detail in chapters 10 and 13.

Digesting the information in this book will enable you to become comfortable with the principal financial terms that make up the language of business. For now, just be assured that knowing your numbers will be a huge help in understanding and meeting the needs of your business. We'll save the details for the "clock" section.

Stay Informed

The mantra of successful business-minded owners could well be "Stay Informed." The natural thought process of therapists is not typically business minded, and thus, many in the field want to avoid or minimize the importance of financial information. Going over a financial statement or planning for the taxes that may be due the following month may feel like too much of a grind. In business there's an old saying that goes like this: "I can take good news. I can take bad news. I cannot take no news." Stay informed. Know how much money is coming in, how much money is going out, and how the money is being used. Even if you have a biller or a bookkeeper handling your finances, you need to know what's going on in your business. Don't assume someone else is taking good care of your money. Your accountant will come in after the fact; your job is to stay informed about the daily, weekly, and monthly financial information.

As I write this, I'm reminded of how many professionals are too trusting of their bookkeepers/billers/office personnel and mistakenly believe that no one would steal from them. We have all heard about doctors, dentists, attorneys, and therapists who delegate all of the money handling to one person in the office. Just this week, a good friend of mine in the medical field shared with me that his bookkeeper had taken off out of the country with a lot of his money. He could never figure out why he hadn't seemed to be getting ahead financially. He worked hard and had appropriate fees but never seemed to have any money. Now he knows why. Very sad.

At this point you may feel somewhat overwhelmed as you consider the financial numbers in your business and the need to stay informed. I understand that this is a bit like learning a new language. But not to worry—I will teach you what you'll need to know in a logical format, building on each item one step at a time.

Secure Feedback Information

As you now know, you'll need to filter the business decisions you make through the question of how those expenses impact your revenue. The money numbers you're about to meet and befriend are going to give you information that will assist you in making wiser financial decisions. As an example, we have all decided at some point that we need a new car—maybe not a brand-new car, but a newer car. By securing the feedback information our numbers provide, we get a realistic picture of the amount we can spend on this purchase. We can calculate the financial implications of a new car and decide whether it's best to lease or purchase the car based on our cash flow and current overhead. (We will discuss overhead and cash flow in part 2, "Clock Issues.")

You may be relieved to learn that business-minded owners look further than just at the numbers. Sometimes you can utilize observations and input from others to make the business more successful or comfortable for all involved. For example, we had an ongoing problem in our office that we hadn't taken the time to resolve. Each night the last one to leave would lock up and set the alarm, but the therapists would keep their doors closed, making it impossible to know who was still in session. That led to people being locked in and triggering the alarm when they left. Our bookkeeper came up with the solution: we started hanging signs on our doors to let people know if we were still in the office working.

Write and Track Goals

The concept of having a business mind-set brings to my mind a client I worked with many years ago. The young man was professionally successful, which, he said, had much to do with his system for tracking and staying focused on his goals. In his computer he kept a spreadsheet that included the categories of goals he wanted to work on: professional, personal, financial, physical, and so on. He listed his goals under appropriate categories and set time frames of thirty, sixty, or ninety days or one year, three years, or five years, and so on. Every two weeks he set aside a specific time to review his progress on each one of his goals. He explained that that way, they were always in the forefront of his mind. When he had decisions to make, he would first ask himself the following question: how will this bring me closer to achieving my goals? Ultimately, he attributed much of his own success to his faithful utilization of his goal-setting and goal-tracking system.

In summary, know your business objectives. I suggest that you write them down, include bench marks that will measure your progress, review them regularly, and celebrate your accomplishments. You may want to increase the number of sessions you do each week, or perhaps you may want to reduce the number of sessions but increase the fee you charge. Many business owners set a specific profit target that they want to meet each year or set a specific goal, like owning their office building. Perhaps your goal is bigger—maybe it's to build a group practice with many clinicians working for you. Regardless of the goal you set, review it regularly, and measure your progress.

3

MENTAL HEALTH CARE: BOTTOM OF THE TOTEM POLE

As Becky was about to discover, an in-depth understanding of money matters and one's mental health care practice goes beyond personal beliefs and skills. It requires an exploration of the beliefs held within the broad mental health field as well as an exploration of those in the larger community of people and organizations that utilize or otherwise deal with mental health care professionals. This discussion focuses on the expectations of the practitioners themselves, the overall attitudes that prevail in mental health care, and, going further afield, the attitudes of those who determine the compensation practitioners receive.

The Altruism Complication

Many people both within the profession and outside of it have the idea that somehow, therapists should perform their work based on their love for it and the compassion they have for people in need. This is often referred to as the statue-of-liberty syndrome based on a phrase engraved on the statue, "Give me your tired, your poor, your huddled masses." Not surprisingly, the compassion implicit in that phrase complicates many therapists' attitude toward being well compensated for their work. After listening to clients who are struggling financially, some therapists decide that those clients need money more than they do; consequently, they fail to set a fee commensurate with the services they provide. *Being a compassionate therapist does not preclude you from being well compensated for your work.*

The expectation is that professionals in this field will care for the huddled masses at a minimum expense to clients, families, insurance companies, agencies, hospitals, and governments or other governing bodies that control the level of care of the mentally/emotionally disturbed members of society. Mental health professionals are vulnerable to this line of thinking, in part because an attraction to the field reflects a deep concern for other people. It's not uncommon for practitioners to have personal experiences with emotional disturbances, whether those experiences are with family members, other loved ones, or even internal conflicts. Those experiences contribute to a strong desire to assist those living with the pain of mental illness.

Right Brains at Work

Adding to the compassionate nature common among mental health professionals is the fact that they're likely to be governed by the right brain, the part that deals comfortably with emotions and the issues that spring from them. Indeed, some clinicians would probably work for free if it were possible to do so. People whose actions are dominated by the left brain have no trouble imagining almost everything on an Excel spreadsheet, but that analytical pattern of thinking is far removed from those whose actions are dominated by the right brain. Right-brain thinkers are uncomfortable looking at therapy as a business, and that makes it easier for them to accept the collective thinking that mental health care professionals do not need to be well paid.

Governing Bodies

The expectation of altruism in treatment is further abetted by the actions of governing bodies. Many states, when striving to balance their budgets, look almost immediately to ways to reduce or even to eliminate funds for mental health care. That leaves professionals in the field facing the challenge of providing services to those in need but with fewer resources to use to work toward their goals. The question that naturally arises, then, is how professionals in the field can balance an expectation to be well paid for their expertise with the collective unconscious that supports the expectation that they should offer their help at a minimum expense.

Measuring Success

Yet another stumbling block is built into the structure of the field of mental health care. Every clinician faces this issue when a client or a client's family member asks the seemingly innocent question, "What is your success rate?" Of course, what they're actually asking is, "Can you fix me?" (Or in the case of a client's family member, "Can you fix my loved one?") Obviously, no clinician can guarantee that a "fix" will take place. Unlike dentists, who can relieve pain by pulling a tooth, those in the mental health field cannot offer such a promise. Some clients come to therapy expecting magic, but all practitioners know that change requires effort, time, and practice—and then more effort, time, and practice. Clinicians provide therapy, coaching, instructions, empathy, motivation, and guidance, but it remains up to the client to do the work that will allow him or her to reap the benefits of therapy. And so when clinicians face the can-you-fix-me question, there is no one clear-cut answer. An issue of integrity arises because while practitioners cannot guarantee the success of their work, in no way does that—or indeed, in no way should it—affect their expectation of payment.

Happily, there are changes coming in the fields of mental health care, therapy, and brain science that are likely to make it possible to one day demonstrate the success of therapy in a more scientific manner. As research has made clear, the past belief that human brains couldn't change after a certain age was proved to be wrong. Not only does neuroplasticity inform us that the brain can and does change, but neuroscientists are also studying how the process of therapy changes an individual's brain. Therapy, with its focus on positive emotions, building empathy, mindfulness, clarifying emotions, and encouraging healthy lifestyles, provides clients with the opportunity to build new neurons (neurogenesis); in other words, it provides them with the opportunity to literally rewire their brains.

Even so, the issue of success will always go back to the clients. Clinicians can have wonderful expertise as therapists and can build an excellent rapport with their clients, but clients' participation and willingness to commit to healing and to participate and fulfill their role in the process have a huge impact on the potential outcome. Regardless of how much future research on therapy and the brain supports the field or of how extensive that research is, success will always be determined by the actions and determination of one's clients. That cannot change.

Mental Health Care: Bottom of the Totem Pole

Mental health care is still "the new kid on the block." It was just over one hundred years ago that Sigmund Freud first introduced the concept of psychotherapy as a way to address emotional and mental disturbances. The field continues to evolve and grow, and the perspective of society continues to shift toward recognizing the value of psychotherapy as well as the education, skills, and expertise required of the effective mental health clinician.

In the meantime, we mental health professionals have a responsibility to make certain that we address our own negative thoughts, emotions, fears, and self-defeating behaviors that feed our negative energies. Negative energies block the potential positive growth that can come from positive energy. As members of a field of practice, our positive beliefs and energies can influence the way we see ourselves and the way we're seen by our clients, our peers, our naysayers, and our supporters. Maintaining positive beliefs and energies must be our commitment to ourselves and to this work we do.

Becky and I completed our exploration of the cloud issues that mental health care professionals must make their way through. At times these issues can feel as enveloping as a dense fog, but an understanding of them and clarity about them will lead to a bright-blue sky with just wisps of clouds high in the sky.

PART 2: CLOCK ISSUES

4

SETTING THE STAGE FOR YOUR BUSINESS

Problems that go *tick-tock, tick-tock* day after day, week after week, and month after month, on and on, are what I refer to as "clock" problems. Running a successful business includes setting up procedures, policies, and tasks that require attention on a regular basis. Establishing these procedures in an organized and clear manner allows the person responsible for doing the tasks to do them in a satisfactory manner and also provides valuable information to you, the professional. A failure to understand clock problems and to establish consistent methods to manage them can result in overwhelming amounts of work, a loss of time, and frustration down the road.

When I think of clock problems, I'm reminded of a good friend of mine who keeps her home extremely well organized. Curious as to how she does that with her busy life, I asked her about it. She explained that she's sure to clean out one drawer every day. By consistently doing a little bit, she avoids the overwhelming task of cleaning out and organizing all of the drawers in her house at the same time. One drawer a day. *Tick-tock, tick-tock.*

5

PRIVATE PRACTICE: THINGS YOU NEED TO KNOW

In one of our many conversations, Becky remarked that when she decided to open her private therapy practice, she was completely clueless about the details she would need to address. Becky said that while she had wonderful therapy training and skills, she was totally unprepared for her role as the CEO of her own business. She added in passing that it would have been a great help to have had a list of what she needed to know and needed to do before she had her first client.

"You know—something like 'five things you must do to set up your therapy business,'" she said with a laugh. "I really could have used that."

Becky's comment got me thinking about what I would include on such a list. I thought too about adding to it a list of things that a new business owner can do to make the entire experience easier and more pleasant.

I've broken my thoughts down into a five-things list, a three-things list, and a one-thing statement. These lists will be helpful to anyone who will be setting up a business or starting a private practice and to anyone who's now in private practice and wants to grow the business to be more successful.

The Five-Things List
What You Must Do to Set Up Your Therapy *Business*

One: Plan a Budget

The first clock issue involves creating a document that demonstrates how you want your business to play out. You need to show how much income you expect to take in and the expenses you expect to have. Consider this warning, though: typically, new businesses overestimate income and underestimate expenses. Initially, you'll be working with estimates, and admittedly, it can be difficult to anticipate income and expenses without hard data, but approach this as realistically as you possibly can.

Expenses fall into two categories: **fixed** and **variable**. Fixed expenses are those you're obligated to pay, such as rent and your phone bill. Obviously, you'll want to keep those expenses as low as possible. To get a good idea of what expenses you'll have and the price range for these expenses, talk with others in the field who are in private practice. With good planning, you can usually anticipate and plan for expenses in a professional office. (For help with this concept, see chapter 9, which is totally devoted to dissecting business expenses.) Unsurprisingly, the greater difficulty is anticipating income.

Most practitioners find that it takes several years to build a therapy practice that will cover the overhead and provide the desired income. To get through those years, you'll need to anticipate how to meet your financial needs so that you can give the business time to grow. Some people are able to rely on the reserve accounts that they've set aside for this purpose; others look to supplement their income with outside work. It's extremely helpful to keep overhead (business expenses) as low as possible until you have a positive cash flow—that is, more money coming in than going out—securely in place.

Rent is one of the biggest items on the expense list. When selecting a home for the business, cost is a major factor, but it's certainly not the only one. We'll now explore some of the other factors to consider when you're in search of an office.

Two: Establish the Right Home for Your Business

Location is one of the most important considerations in selecting an office—and it potentially relates to how expensive your rent will be as well. Here are factors to keep in mind as you go through listings.

Consider the impact of the size of the community you'll be practicing in. If you'll be part of a small community, your location will likely be convenient to just about every potential client. However, in a larger community, people tend to want a therapist who's conveniently located to their home or business. Keep in mind the population you want to attract to your business; once you've identified your target demographic, you can search for an office in an area that's convenient for that group.

The next consideration concerns how many mental health practices are already in the area. If the neighborhood is saturated with them, and the population density can't support that many, it just makes sense to look elsewhere.

The question of incorporating a professional office into the home is a common one. Initially, a home office looks appealing; it keeps expenses down and is obviously convenient for the therapist as well. But be warned there are downsides to a home office.

First of all, having a home office may not be legal in your

community or in your homeowners association. Many communities and HOAs have laws or rules against it unless the area is specifically zoned for such a business. Also check to see whether you'll be able to obtain a business license for a home-based business. If you're legally allowed to practice in your home and can get a business license, how will you keep your personal and family life separate from your business? Having a private entrance for clients and setting your office away from the rest of the house could provide enough separation for both you and your clients to be comfortable. After all, having your clients walk through your personal residence and see your family members and personal household items is hardly professional. There's also the question of confidentiality if family members or neighbors see your clients. Then there's safety to consider. As mental health professionals, we deal with a wide range of people and problems. Having a home office could place you in a vulnerable and potentially dangerous situation. If you're set on having a home office, I advise that at the very least, you screen potential clients at another location before accepting them into your home.

Single Office or Group Practice

An excellent place to rent office space is in an established mental health practice. Someone else has already put in the work of constructing an office with a furnished waiting room; separate therapy offices; and a workroom with copy and fax machines, a microwave, and a refrigerator. Sharing the expenses incurred in a larger office also lowers each individual renter's costs, making it a win-win situation for everyone. Many offices accept renters looking for space on a part-time basis as long as they're willing to share that office with another part-time worker.

Group practices, though, are not all alike. In some of them, all of the therapists are solo practitioners. Such groups offer no group-name marketing, no group training, few group meetings, little or no possibility of sharing clients, and no shared liability.

On the other hand, there are groups in which renters become a member of a formal group. In those cases, advertising, websites, and marketing are all done under the group name. Typically, those groups have weekly business meetings with clinical discussions and presentations. The group may handle money as a whole, with clinicians receiving a percentage of the earnings after the office overhead is covered.

Yet another possibility is to join a group practice as an employee of the person who owns the group. These kinds of businesses carry the employees' professional liability insurance and pay the payroll taxes. As an employee, you may be assigned clients, and the owner may track your earnings and submit insurance claims as well as collect payments from clients. Salary is sometimes based on an hourly basis and sometimes is a percentage of the revenue earned.

Finally, for those professionals who want their own office space but can't afford the rent involved, renting in a professional office suite might be the solution. As a rule, these offices provide a front-desk receptionist and office equipment such as copy and fax machines. Keep in mind, though, that patient confidentiality could be an issue: will clients need to walk through the suite of offices, and is there sufficient soundproofing to assure that sessions will be kept private?

Offices specifically built for therapy practices have additional soundproofing between offices, separate cold-air returns, solid doors with soundproofing strips on the bottom, and a locked door between the waiting room and the therapy offices. Professional office suites seldom have those features. Additionally, remember that therapists often have work hours that extend past the usual business day and sometimes have weekend appointments. Most professional buildings do not provide for any hours other than the usual business hours (i.e., Monday through Friday, eight in the morning to five at night).

Regardless of the group arrangement you choose, look for professionals who are ethical, polite, friendly, and supportive of one another. The therapy business can be a stressful and lonely experience and is made more difficult if the group of practitioners in the office have problems getting along or create animosity among their peers. Every mental health professional has had the experience of needing a hug after a particularly difficult session. It is nice to have someone there who understands and willingly offers that hug.

My business partner and I have been together for over twenty years, a fact that gave rise to the joke that we've lasted longer than many marriages. In addition to our two offices, our office space includes a waiting room, a kitchen/workroom, a bathroom, a private back door, and six additional offices that we rent out to other therapists.

While we have a wonderfully compatible and supportive group of clinicians in our office, there are occasional problems among them. We have found that most problems typically result from clinicians' sharing an office space. Issues run the gamut from someone not ending a session on time and thus blocking the other therapist from starting a session promptly to someone leaving shoes that others find malodourous in the office. Disagreements sometimes erupt over bathroom usage, food left in the fridge, timely rent payments, someone speaking to someone else's client in the waiting room, and, of course, increases in rent. We frequently find that clinicians want access to their offices twenty-four-seven but only want to pay part-time rent. Of course, it doesn't work that way. If your budget allows for it, I recommend renting an office full time with a compatible group.

Three: Bureaucratic Stuff

There are government and agency requirements that you must handle when starting up any new business. I have provided a list of them. Different states and provinces have different requirements, but you can use this list to check out the requirements in your area. Some items on the list are self-explanatory; others require some description.

Business Structure

Business structure refers to the type of entity under which you're establishing your business. There are four main entities used in the United States. They are sole proprietorships, limited liability companies (LLC), S corporations, and C corporations.

Most mental health professionals start out as a sole proprietorship. A sole proprietorship is the easiest and least complicated entity and has few special requirements. A sole proprietor reports income and expenses to the Internal Revenue Service on his or her personal 1040 tax return. The IRS has a special form, the schedule C, that's used for this purpose. (There's more information on this topic in chapter 16.)

Moving on from a sole proprietorship calls for a consultation with your accountant about how to convert your business into a more complex entity (either an LLC or a corporation). For example, an entity change would be appropriate if you want to create a greater separation between you and the business for liability purposes. A therapist with a growing business and a number of employees might also want to make this change.

The EIN, or the Federal Employer Identification Number

The US government assigns an EIN to each business. Even if you don't have employees and as such are not technically an employer, your business still needs its own number. Insurance companies recognize you by your EIN, and they report income paid to your business with this number. The advantage here is that you can avoid giving your social security number to insurance companies. Your business bank account will also be attached to your EIN number. Think of the EIN as your business's personal ID number, just as your social security number is your personal government number.

The application process to receive an EIN is simple, and you can apply online. The form will first ask you to identify your business entity. You must decide what type of business entity you are before you apply for an EIN. (See the above discussion on business entities.)

DBA, or "Doing Business As"

Instead of using your personal name as the name of your business, you have the option to select a name that says something about what you do or where you're located. South Hill Family Counseling, Loving Hearts Therapy, and Marriage Rescue Center are all examples of DBAs.

There are three main reasons you'll want to select a more generic, professional sounding name. The first reason is that a business name different from your name does lend an air of professionalism to your business. The second reason is that the domain name of your website will sound more professional. The third reason is that when the time comes for you to retire and to sell your business, you'll have a business with a name that is well known and respected in your community. If your business name is your personal name, when you're no longer affiliated with the business, its value could easily decrease, making it a less desirable purchase.

Register your business name (your DBA name) with the county clerk's office, which will typically charge you a small fee. To prevent your DBA name from being confused with another business—for example, your South Hill Counseling Center could be confused with the South Hill Family Counseling Center across the street—register not only the DBA name you've selected but also any other name that is similar to it.

And while you are at it, go online and buy your DBA for your domain name (your URL). You'll need it for your website, which we'll discuss later.

Business License

States, counties, cities, and municipalities have different requirements and procedures for filing for a business license. This information is online. Check out the requirements in your area and complete the necessary paperwork, fees, and filing.

Business Phone

Your options for a business phone service will depend

somewhat on the phone service provided in the office you rent. Some larger groups have a receptionist to answer calls, but many therapists prefer to use cell phones for their professional needs. Have one that's devoted to business only; its number should also be the one that appears on your website, business cards, and other marketing tools.

Texting is a great way for established clients to contact you with a short message when they need to change an appointment or tell you that they're running late. Texting is not a problem if you have a devoted business cell phone; if you don't, give your personal number to clients for texting only and explain that for longer messages or voice messages, they should use e-mail or call the office number.

Business Cards

Once you have your address, phone number, and business name, you'll be ready to get your business cards printed. You'll find many designs to choose from in online services, or you may want to have a logo designed for you.

Professional Bank Account

It's best not to combine your business and personal bank accounts. Keeping them separate makes it much easier to track income and expenses. Be sure to open a savings account when you set up your business account.

Business Credit Card

It'll be easier to track your credit card business expenses if you set one specific card aside for business use. Make only business purchases on this card.

Professional Insurances

As a therapist and a business owner, you're required to have certain forms of insurance, and having others is advisable too. You must have professional liability insurance. Renter's insurance is recommended for office-space rentals. A business-renter insurance policy will cover the items in your office in case of fire, a theft, or another destructive force as well as in the case of injuries that result from an accident in your office. It's a good idea to consider disability insurance as well. None of us like to think about something bad happening and interfering with work, but as a self-employed person, you need to consider how you would pay your expenses should you have a debilitating injury or an illness. Read the details of these policies carefully, as coverage can be spotty and complex.

Shop around to various insurance companies to find a reputable insurance professional and a stable insurance company you're comfortable doing business with. A good agent will be able to explain the various options and costs of these types of policies.

Three: Policies and Procedures

As if being the CEO weren't enough, you will now be responsible for operations—that is, how your office functions. That makes you the chief operations officer, or the "COO," the person who handles the policies, procedures, and organizational structure of the business. If you're a mental health clinician setting up a private practice, something as simple as how you manage incoming phone calls will affect the success of your business. What is an acceptable amount of time between receiving a message on voice mail and returning the call? Even in so-called "paperless" offices, you'll still have office paperwork that requires organization. Consider, for example, intake forms, client contracts, insurance forms, client files, session schedules, and information about incoming calls and responses to calls returned. These documents are in addition to the paperless files you keep on each client. Money issues, however, including reporting income, paying bills, filing insurance claims, and making bank deposits, are not jobs on the COO's to-do list. Money is the job of the CFO, or the "chief financial officer." And yes, that's also your job. (You'll find a lot more information on money in the chapters that follow.)

Professional Intake Forms

Future clients will need to complete a number of forms before their first session, either online or in the waiting room at the time of their initial appointment. You can simplify this task by having intake forms on your website along with information about you and your practice; the added bonus is that that practice will increase traffic to your website. You'll find many intake forms online; to determine what makes up a good intake form, consider information in two categories: the first is the information you need to know about this new client, and the second is the information your client needs to know about you and your expectations of him or her.

Information the Client Provides

Let's look first at the information that will be necessary and useful for you to have. Obviously, you'll need the client's demographic and personal information: name; address; phone numbers (including the preferred phone number for your calls or messages and whether you have permission to text him or her); e-mail address; age; date of birth; employment status; employer; marital status (and number of years married if applicable); number of children in and out of the home; emergency contact information; referral source; and primary and secondary insurance. The questionnaire can also ask for information such as the client's health; medications; use of alcohol or drugs; prior therapy experiences; psychological symptoms, current and past; suicidality; history of suicide attempts; family members' psychological conditions; and current major stresses. It is helpful to ask on the intake form what the client hopes to accomplish in therapy and what has prompted him or her to seek therapy.

During the session that follows, you'll ask the client to expand on the information he or she provided and to discuss it with you. It will be useful for you to have the form in hand and to build on it as the session progresses.

Information You Provide: The Therapy Contract

The client is entering a contractual agreement with you, the therapist. It is important to clearly state and discuss all relevant information and to have the appropriate papers/forms signed. Here we'll look at the information you're required and advised to provide to the client. Again, you'll find excellent resources online that will provide you with ideas about how to structure this contract.

The **consent-to-services/rights-acknowledgment** contract addresses the fact that the client agrees to therapy and understands the roles of the therapist and the client. The client's rights include the right to enter therapy by free choice and to terminate it at any time. When you agree to accept the client into your practice, the client can assume appointments will be readily available. If you cannot meet the need of regularly scheduled appointments, make that clear to the client when you accept him or her. The client also has the right to expect all aspects of the therapy to remain confidential, and any exceptions of confidentiality need to be clearly stated and understood by the client.

The financial aspects of the therapy agreement include the fee per session, the acceptable methods of payment, and the client's insurance benefits as well as how those benefits impact the money you'll collect at the time of session. You must also list and explain additional fees for such items as court appearances, depositions, school visits as a part of the therapy process, sessions with family members with or without the client, group sessions, fees for phone calls with the therapist between sessions, and fees for special reports.

Although it won't be explicitly stated in the consent-to-services contract, the client will have the expectation that the therapist will abide by the ethical rules that govern the clinician's license. Most clients are aware of the ethical expectations of confidentiality and of the lack of intimacy between the therapist and the client, but they may be less familiar with professional boundaries that continue after the therapy is completed. It is wise to explain that confidentiality and professional boundaries continue to exist even after therapy is completed.

A HIPAA Notice of Privacy Practices must be made available to your client. A form acknowledging that the client has been advised of the HIPAA Privacy Practices, which the client needs to sign, must be included in the client file.

Cancellations and no-shows are always a concern in a therapy business. As noted in another chapter, the client purchases an hour of your time when making an appointment. You will need to determine your policies about clients' rescheduling or cancelling appointments. Do you require twenty-four-hour, forty-eight-hour, or day-before notice to change an appointment? What is the fee you charge for a late cancelation or a no-show? To avoid any misunderstandings in the future, be sure to address your cancellation/reschedule policy at the first session with your client; even though the client contract clearly states your policy, discussing it directly with the client will solidify the information for him or her.

Many clients sign the forms without bothering to read the information. That makes it necessary to review the most important points during the first session in order to be certain that they understand the conditions of and expectations for therapy. The first session is also a good time to address any questions the clients may have and to provide any necessary clarifications.

Five: Website and Marketing

It isn't enough to be the professional clinician, the CEO, the COO, and the CFO in your business. Now you must also be the Webmaster and the marketing executive.

A website is vital for any business in today's world. It's how people find you, how they learn about you, how they get to know you, and how they decide if you're the person they want to sit down with and tell their story to.

It is well worth the money to have an expert design and build your website. In their search through the Internet for the right professional, potential clients will judge you instantly by your site. Be sure that the site speaks directly to your target market and that it tells people exactly what you do and why you would be a good choice to be their therapist.

Marketing has become a huge industry. Fortunately, there are professional people who are well trained and have years of experience who can help you market and build the kind of practice you want. In addition to building a website, there are several things you can do to start getting your name out there and making yourself known.

Many local groups seek out speakers for lunch meetings. Contact those organizations and propose topics of interest to them that you're prepared to cover in a presentation. Think about titles in the same way that magazines like *TMZ* think about their headlines. The titles of your presentations should grab people's attention, make them curious, and leave them wanting more.

But consider this warning about marketing: be sure to track your return on investment (ROI). If you decide to put together a booth at a bridal convention as a marketing tool for your business, you'll want to figure out how many new clients and appointments you scheduled as a result of that expense. That is tracking the return on your investment. The money you pay for your website or to a professional marketer should also be tracked. You should expect it to come back to you as a significant increase of earnings coming into your business.

It is always helpful to find out how potential clients heard about you. Most of the people who call me say either that they found me on the Internet or that someone referred me to them.

Fortunately, you can go online to find an abundance of material available for therapists about how to market and build a business. Spend some time looking through some of the many ways people market their businesses. Create and implement a marketing plan for yourself based on the ideas you learn online.

Since this is a book about money matters for therapists, I present only the return on investment (ROI) aspect of spending money to make money. You have to do it. Bite the bullet, and eat mac and cheese if necessary, but get a good professional website.

6
THINGS THAT MAKE YOUR LIFE EASIER

One: Software

Again, this book is about money—specifically, it's about your money, how to manage your money, and how to get more money. So, you may ask, what does software have to do with my money? The answer is a lot.

The first software that I strongly recommend you purchase, install, and start using *today* is some type of money software. This software will relieve you of the task of having to organize many, indeed most, of the details required for successful money management.

I have been using Quicken for many years. It serves my needs, it's not expensive, it's easy to use, and it backs up automatically upon request. The home and business version of Quicken provides important financial statements for your business and categorizes business expenses for your income taxes' schedule C. I rely on my Quicken software to provide me with all of the financial information I require to evaluate the numbers in my business, and it is user friendly. You do not have to put all of your financial statements together. A good money software program will do that for you as long as you've entered your financial information correctly.

There are more complex and expensive money-management software packages, but it's unlikely that you'll need anything that complicated. Software such as QuickBooks is actually intended for bookkeepers and accountants. It's better to have something really user friendly and not to pay more money for a program that overwhelms you and that you do not need.

In addition to looking for something user friendly and fairly priced, look for a software program that tracks all of your income, expenses, and payables. This book will teach you which financial statements you'll need to review and how important and informative those statements will be as you run your business. Regardless of the software you select, be sure it prepares a bank-reconciliation statement, a profit-and-loss statement, a cash-flow statement, and a balance sheet. Once you become accustomed to using your software, you'll wonder how you ever got along without it.

Other software programs worth exploring include some of the therapy-practice software that have recently become available. Life is getting better for therapists. Now, if the right software is connected to your website, established clients can go online and schedule an appointment, complete all of their paperwork, or cancel or reschedule an appointment. They can do all of that while you're in session with someone else. That software saves time, is efficient, and, in the long run, will save you money. Although I personally do not (yet) use that software, I have looked into it and have spoken with a number of therapists who do use it. Three software programs I have heard good things about are Simple Practice, TheraNest Mental Health, and Therapy Partner.

Billing software, online submissions for insurance payments, and direct deposits from insurance practices to one's bank all make doing business more convenient. These tools free up our time and allow us to have sessions, do marketing, educate others, give a speech at a newcomers' luncheon, or go to lunch with a friend to enjoy some refreshing "me time."

Some therapist software includes the option to enter all client files into your computer. Doing so removes the need to have client files in your office. Frankly, I find it difficult to consider using this particular aspect of the software, because I keep client notes with graphs, drawings, geometry (triangulating), and other such methods that would be difficult to enter into my PC. It's possible to use this option, but I suspect it's not for me.

When considering what software you want to use, be wary of spending too much on it. Remember, keep your overhead low. Some packages come with monthly fees, which can make the cost of the software more manageable, but be sure that the fees are easily within your budget.

And here's one final thought: back up your data. Some software including Quicken comes with the option to use the cloud to back up all data. There are also a number of services that can arrange cloud storage that backs up regularly and automatically. If, though, you prefer an external hard drive, back up your data daily, and take that hard drive home with you every night. I can't even think about the concept of losing one client file, and if I lost all my client files…

Two: People

As you've probably figured out by now, you're operating a business that has many pieces. Can you manage them all by yourself? Well, perhaps if you're willing to give up sleep, eating (except at your desk), and hanging out with the people in your life who you really like—like your kids, your spouse, or your friends. You know—those people.

So what to do?

Hire people. Evaluate everything you do or would like to do in a two- or four-week period. What are you doing that you could hand over to someone else, thus opening your schedule to do one more session or one more marketing event? I started by hiring a biller/bookkeeper to manage all of the insurance billing, insurance authorizations, client ledgers, and monthly/annual summary-of-earnings statements. She is not my employee. She has her own medical-billing/bookkeeping business. Even though I could do all of that work myself, spending hours doing billing when I could be in session would be a poor utilization of my earning potential.

You also have the option to hire a virtual assistant to help you manage your business. There are many types of assistants you can hire online, including those you can hire for a specific project such as updating your LinkedIn site and those you can hire for a longer period of time to do other administrative work for you. A virtual assistant could be working on your Facebook ad or LinkedIn account while you're in session earning at least five times what you pay that person. Hiring an assistant is about maximizing your time and energy and increasing your profits. Virtual-assistant services are located inside the United States as well as in other countries.

Three: Retirement Account

Many of us think that we'll continue to work until we are hauled off to the nursing home or that other place. But in truth, most of us would eventually like the option of working fewer days a week or possibly of not working at all. Furthermore, a changing health condition could be a reason to rethink one's work schedule. As such, doing some financial planning to create a safety net is not only wise but also necessary. If you can start your retirement account early in your professional life, you'll find there are huge advantages to doing so. The more years your money can grow, the greater the return on your investment will be.

The type of retirement accounts you set up will depend in part on the type of entity you formed for your business. Discuss this with your financial adviser, and make a promise to yourself that you'll fund your account on a regular basis. Then do it. Of course, there will be times when you'd rather use that money for something else, but saving for retirement is not an optional expense. It is mandatory. Be a smart investor, and have your financial adviser detail all of the fees and costs associated with your retirement account. Watch for hidden fees that can take a huge bite out of your hard-earned money, thereby significantly diminishing the returns you get.

7

AND FINALLY, THE *ONE* THING YOU WILL BE REALLY GLAD YOU DID

I'll give you a hint: it has to do with money, planning, paying bills, feeling comfortable, enhancing your ability to relax, and being more confident about your business. You're no doubt wondering what could possibly make that big of a difference in your life. Well, as a fellow business owner, I know you worry. You worry about paying the rent on time, about paying the utilities, and about paying the phone bill so clients won't hear the message, "this is no longer a working number." (Now that would be embarrassing—although, of course, you would point to a phone company mix-up.) You worry about having enough appointments this month to pay all of your bills. You worry when checks from insurance companies don't arrive in a timely fashion (which they seldom do, especially in January.) You worry. And all that worry takes away from your focus and concentration while you're in session. Presence, attunement, empathy—oh my. Add to all of that your worries about whether the lights will still be on when that client (hopefully) returns the next week. This is tough stuff. So what to do?

The answer is so simple I'm almost embarrassed to let you

in on it. Can you do it overnight? *No*. But with careful planning, you can make it happen, and your life will get much easier, and you will worry a lot less. How wonderful—how fabulous—to be free of worries about money!

I can't do anything about your teenagers or your spouse, but I can help you with your money management.

What if at the *beginning* of each month, you looked at your money-management software account and saw that you had a balance of $10,000 in your bank account? I imagine that would feel pretty good. And, even better, what if you knew (because you'd been tracking your expenses) that you needed a total of $8,900 to cover the bills and your owner's draw for the coming month?

"Hmm," you think. "That means I would have money left over at the end of the month. But wait. We're at the beginning of the month. That means that all the money that comes in this month won't have to be spent on this month's bills. Oh! That means that at the end of the month, there will be enough in the bank account to pay next month's bills, and I won't have to worry about paying one single bill late. Wow! That feels really good."

So here's the plan: Pay this month's bills with last month's earnings. And, even better, build up your cash account so that it has two or three months' earnings in it with which you can pay the current month's bills. That is freedom!

But remember this simple word of caution: Do not leave that extra money in your checking account. It's far too easy to spend the money that's left in there by spending a little here and a little there. No. Move the money into the savings account and out of your sight.

As we move into the "clock" items of business, we will cover a lot of information that will put you in charge of your money. To do so is a matter of establishing patterns in your life and of taking care of what you need to do, even if that means doing the same things again and again. *Tick-tock.*

8

Introducing the Numbers: A Brief Interlude Before We Meet Them

A dear friend of mine is a magnificent photographer, a professor of photography, and a photo consultant. She was hired by a major software company to review their online photo collection. During her first meeting with the software techies, she asked to see their photo collection of "time." The software engineers proudly opened up their file of photos marked "time." There on the screen were photos of clocks. Lots and lots of clocks. What says "time" to a computer techie more than a clock?

When my friend shared this experience with me, she said, "I knew I had earned my consultant fee right then and there." The idea of seeing time from a metaphorical perspective had not occurred to even one of those bright young techies. Those dominant left-brain thinkers thought of time as a clock. My friend's artist brain could immediately produce images of time that opened up the minds of those engineers and allowed them to see it from a new perspective. She showed them photos of a child's hand in an old, worn one; photos of space; and photos of sunrises and sunsets. And then more and more photos all demonstrating time came bursting forth on her computer screen.

And so it is with you and the numbers in your business. You are not an accountant, nor would you ever aspire to become one. Your right brain would become exhausted from having to get all of those numbers exactly right and then having to make them exactly match the bottom of the page. "How tedious," you would say. Your natural tendency is to be comfortable discussing the "cloud" issues concerning money, as we did in the part 1. But these "clock" issues—real numbers—likely create some feelings of unease for you.

I am hoping that just as my friend demonstrated another perspective of time to the computer techies, this book will present you with another perspective of how you can become comfortable with the numbers of business. My goal is to present each concept in a way that is useful, practical, direct, and understandable. My bigger goal is that as a result of implementing these functions in your business, it will grow and become wildly successful.

I have spoken with many therapists about their reluctance to implement solid financial principles in their businesses. My concerns for each one of them were that they didn't know what they didn't know and that they were building on a business model that is less successful and more stressful than necessary.

If you follow the steps I outline in this book, you'll see how numbers tell the story of your business. The numbers are like characters in a book, and you are the author. Every number in your business has a name, a message, and an important role to play in the functions and success of your business. I'm going to introduce you to the main characters, the major players. These are the important numbers, and you'll soon learn what each one means, how each one be-

Introducing the Numbers:
A Brief Interlude before We Meet Them

haves when times are good, and how each one behaves when times are not so great. And since you're the author of your numbers, you'll learn what you can do to get your numbers to tell a wonderful, fulfilling success story.

As you become more comfortable hanging out with these numbers, you'll begin to see their patterns. That will help you predict what they'll do next. You will spot warning signs of danger ahead. This next point deserves a "drum roll": there may be incidents of the numbers not getting along, at which point you'll realize that you need to make some changes.

There will also be times when you will celebrate with your numbers. Cheers to all!

These numbers are your friends. Get to know each one. Eventually, you'll reach a place where you know that the numbers are behaving in the way that works best for you—the way that brings you the kind of peace that lets you sleep at night knowing your business numbers are at their best. That is the place I call "financial savvy."

And now, on to the numbers.

9

IT COSTS HOW MUCH?
OVERHEAD

I recently met up with a therapist-friend from years ago, a woman I had once worked with. In catching up on each other's lives and professional growth, I told her that I was writing a book on finances for mental health care professionals. She responded by saying that she wished she'd had a book like that thirty years ago.

"Life would have been much easier," she added with a sigh. Then she explained to me that in all of the years she'd been in practice (she had retired), she had never once reconciled her bank account or calculated the expenses of her business. She admitted that it had been too distressing for her to figure out how to keep track of her money and that if the numbers had been bad, she wouldn't have known what to do about it. As long as she could pay her bills every month, she said, she didn't concern herself with money and her practice.

Now that she's retired, she often looks back on all of the money she earned and on all of the money she wasted. Never did she view or treat her career as a business. She added that her spouse used to refer to her work as "that little counseling job." Later, as I reflected on our conversation, I wondered if she too had viewed her business as "that little counseling job."

Today's clinicians are working in a very different health business environment than the clinicians of the past. The environment now requires practitioners to know and to utilize solid business principles and practices. Luckily, that doesn't mean that it's necessary to attend accounting classes to learn how to manage the finances in our businesses. What we do need to learn are the basic essentials in business and accounting that relate to our type of business.

Once we have mastered those concepts, we can put systems in place that will enable us to review our financial data, and in doing so, we can become effective managers of our businesses. Whether you're new to private practice, as Becky was, or have been in practice for a number of years, you can see how important it is to know and to understand the numbers in your business.

So let's move on to the numbers of business.

The Cost of Business

The crucial money question we will first tackle is, how much does it cost me to stay in business?

Using the language of business, we can ask the same question in a different way: What is my overhead?

The cost of running a business—that is, the overhead—is a number every business owner needs to know and track. Operating costs can change. Any increase or decrease in one of the expense categories changes the overhead number. Such things as heat in the winter and air conditioning in the summer impact your total expenditure. Fortunately, it is not difficult to keep an eye on your overhead if you review your total monthly expenditures to see if there are any significant changes.

Mental health professionals are in what's broadly referred to as a "service industry." In the language of business, that means that we don't manufacture any items or sell any merchandise in the course of our business. Our earnings come from the services we provide to the people who purchase our services. The expenses we incur in the process of providing these services directly result from our businesses and are called, not surprisingly, *direct expenses*. Other types of businesses, such as manufacturing, have two types of expenses: indirect and direct. I'm explaining this so that if you come across a reference to direct and indirect expenses in business, you'll be familiar with the meaning of the two terms and aware that you need concern yourself only with direct expenses.

Business Expenses

It is important to know what items are considered business expenses. You're allowed to take all of them as deductions on your tax return. I have met many clinicians who haven't deducted all of the allowed expenses on their tax returns and thus have paid more taxes than were necessary.

The key to legitimate business expenses is that they must be expenses that you can prove are both "ordinary and necessary" for the purpose of your business. In other words, these are the expenses you must pay to stay in business. Most of these are payable whether you're in your office working or sitting on a beach in Hawaii.

Even though all of these expenses directly affect your ability to work, there are significant differences between them that are worth exploring. Some expenses, such as rent, are a set amount, and payment for them is due on a specific day. This type of expense is referred to as a "fixed expense." Once you've signed a lease, you're liable for payment every month for the length of the lease.

Another potential fixed expense is the salary you agreed to pay to an employee you hired. Your obligation is to pay the salary, the withholding tax, and the employer's FICA tax by a specific date. If you decide to let that employee go, you will relieve yourself of the fixed expense of salary and taxes, but for as long as that person is your employee, you'll remain responsible for those expenses.

The other type of expense category is called "variable expenses." For our purposes, these are the expenses that we have more control over. We can alter the amounts we spend on the expenses in this category and have some control over when we make the payments for them.

A professional-development expense is a good example of a variable expense. Although we must spend money to obtain the professional continuing-education credits required for our license, there are many options for how much we spend for them. The timing of that expense is also up to us, since we have a full year to earn our credits. Those two factors categorize this expense as a variable one.

I want to include a short note here about the importance of keeping fixed expenses as low as possible, which I've been stressing throughout this book. That idea is crucial because when it comes to fixed expenses, there is no wiggle room. Many businesses get into trouble because they take on too many fixed expenses. High fixed expenses then start to drive the revenue; the pressure to meet the rent and to keep the doors open can easily lead to poor business decisions. Once a business is on this track, it is difficult to recover.

The goal should always be the other way around: revenue should drive expenses—expenses shouldn't drive revenue. When revenue starts to increase, it will be time to start thinking about taking on additional expenses that will generate more income.

There is real value to you, the business owner, in separating your expenses into these two categories. In times of economic downturn, you may need to cut back on your business overhead. The flexibility you will need to decrease your payment obligations will be found in the variable-expense category.

A typical operating-expense list for a professional-service business is likely to include the following expenses. Look over the expenses to determine which ones relate to your business. If you have others that are not on this list, add them in.

Fixed Expenses
- rent
- licenses
- salaries (of employees)
- employer's share of FICA taxes

Variable Expenses
- advertising/marketing/website
- amortization/depreciation
- auto expenses
- bank fees

- communication
- dues
- insurances
- interest
- legal/professional fees
- maintenance/repairs
- meals and entertainment (business)
- office
- professional development
- retirement-fund contribution
- supplies
- taxes (local and property)
- travel (business)
- utilities

Owner's Draw, or Salary

You may have noticed there is no mention of your salary in the list of expenses. As a self-employed sole proprietor, you do not receive one. Those who organize their businesses as corporations do receive a salary that is included in the salary total. But most mental health professionals utilize the sole-proprietor model, so that's the model we'll use for our examples.

A sole proprietor takes money out of the business, a concept that is referred to as "a draw" in the language of business. The draw is not included in calculations of the overhead amount. Nor is it deductible as an expense on your income tax return because it's not part of the business overhead.

Calculating Your Overhead

Figure 9.1 is the list Becky wrote out when she was calculating her business overhead expenses. You'll see that some expenses are missing from her list because she didn't pay those particular expenses. For example, she rented her office space from us, and we paid for the utilities, Wi-Fi, cleaning, in-office land lines, office copy machine, print cartridges, copy-machine supplies, microwave, refrigerator, and fax machine. We have a company website, but Becky opted to have an individual website to use for marketing and blogging. She also had her own cell phone that she used for business.

It is now your turn to calculate your business overhead. To make it easier, you can use the "Overhead Expenses" form in the appendix of this book. Our website also has a copy of this form that you can download and use to calculate your overhead.

To complete the form, list all of your expenses and the amounts you pay for each category over a specific period of time. It is preferable to calculate all of your expenses for a full year. I will address how to make the adjustments necessary for those who haven't been in business for a full year. For the rest of you, let's figure out where you can find these numbers.

If the current year's expenses are very close to those you paid last year, it's fine to use a copy of the self-employment income reporting form—schedule C attached to your 1040—that you filed last tax year. Schedule C lists all of the business expenses paid for a given tax year.

Figure 9.1

Becky's Overhead Expenses

Rent	$12,000
Licenses	$300
Advertising, website	$2,000
Depreciation	$1,000
Auto	$2,500
Bank/Card fees	$1,300
Communication (cell phone and Internet)	$2,400
Dues	$800
Insurances (including health and liability)	$3,800
Interest	$2,000
Legal/professional	$1,200
Meals and entertainment (business)	$800
Professional development	$900
Retirement	$3,000
Supplies	$800
Taxes (business)	$200
Travel	<u>$1,000</u>
Total Annual Overhead Expenses	**$36,000**

If the current tax year is quite different than previous years, you'll need to use up-to-date information. I am hoping that by now, you've installed a money software program, and you or someone you trust is managing your bank account, paying your bills, and depositing your checks. If you have this software set up, you can simply print out a list of all of the expense categories you've paid and the amounts you've paid for each. Since there are expenses you pay only once or twice a year, you'll want to look at the numbers for each month of the year. Do not just take the amount of one month's expenses and multiply it by twelve to calculate annual expense. Our professional license fees, insurance costs, and professional-organization dues are all examples of expenses that are typically paid once a year.

Those who have not been in business for a full year will need to make an educated estimate of what the expenses in the remaining months of the first year will be. You can do that by studying the patterns of your costs, which should provide you with a good idea of how much your expenses for the remaining months of the year will cost and when you'll need to pay them. You already know what your fixed expenses will be, so focus on the variable expenses.

Keep in mind that variable expenses can be quite different from month to month. When you initially set up your office, you probably spent a significant amount of money on supplies. Chances are good that you won't need to spend that much again within any one-month time period. You may not have spent much on marketing yet, but you may be planning for a big marketing project later in the year. Adjust and estimate each category on the list as best you can with the information you have about your business—that is, what you're spending and how much you expect to spend during your first twelve months in business.

Enter the amounts on the sheet you copied from the appendix or from our website. The total of these amounts will give you your overhead number for one year.

It's helpful to see the monthly average of each total expense. Just divide the total number by twelve, and there it is—the amount of money you must earn every month to keep your business doors open.

Becky was surprised when she listed and added up all of the expenses she needed to cover to run her business. Here are Becky's overhead numbers:

Becky's total business expense for
    twelve months: $ 36,000
Becky's average monthly expense: $ 3,000

Now, just as Becky knew her total amounts, you too have your total annual overhead. I wonder what your response is when you look at how much it costs you to stay in business. I imagine that many of you had some idea of what that cost would be. Did you find the figure was more or less than what you'd expected? I would love to hear from you. You can share your findings at our website, www.savvymoneybooks.com.

Typically, there is not a wide variance in monthly overhead. If you see a significant change in it, be sure to explore why it occurred. Perhaps you paid off the new computer system, which means that you can expect your overhead to decrease. If you signed up for an expensive professional training, you can expect your overhead to increase. Part of managing your business is keeping track of your monthly overhead and making certain there's an explanation for any change.

In the next chapter, we'll explore a basic financial statement that will provide you with your overhead amount as well as give you a lot of other valuable information.

10

Meet Your Income Statement

CEOs, CFOs, business owners, and you—all are busy people. In large businesses, the owners have a staff to manage the bank account, collect the money earned (the receivables), pay the expenses (the payables), and manage the various accounting procedures. Income and expense numbers are put together in specific formats and given to the CEO, the CFO, or the business owner on a regular basis for review. These financial statements provide a snapshot of specific, valuable financial information regarding the overall health of the business. The first statement most owners and staff look at—and the one we are going to explore here—is the income statement.

On your money-management software, you will find a list of reports you can run. One of them will be named "the income/expense report" or "the profit-and-loss report," although that report is often referred to more simply as the "income statement." This is the first financial statement you need to understand and to utilize. Once you become knowledgeable about the income statement, you'll appreciate how much useful information you can glean from such a straightforward form.

The Income Statement

The income statement provides specific information about the earnings and the expenses of a company or a business. You'll find there are a number of additional names for this statement. Among the most common are "**revenue statement**"; "**statement of financial performance**"; "**earnings statement**"; "**operating statement**"; "**net-income statement**"; and "**profit-and-loss statement**," which is frequently referred to as the "**P & L.**"

Don't let these names confuse you. Despite the different names, these statements have the same format and the same purpose, and they provide basically the same information. They all report the revenue and expenses of a company over a specific period of time. The last line of each of these statements is the amount of money the business has made (its profit) or the amount of money the company has lost (its loss), thus the name "P & L"—profit and loss.

An income statement is for the specific period of time that is named in the title. For example, you may have a monthly income statement titled "January 1, 2016, through January 31, 2016." The time period represented on the statement is usually a month, a quarter, or a year. If you're running your income statement on a money-software program, you can request any time period you want to see.

The top number on the income statement is the "**total earnings**," or "**total income**," which is also referred to as the "**gross receipts**," or "**gross revenue**." Regardless of which term is used, this number is the amount of money your business collected during a specific period of time. If you're running an annual income statement, that number will reflect the amount of money your business collected for the entire calendar year.

Meet Your Income Statement

Under the earnings number is a list of expenses paid for each category during that year. This list will look similar to the one you prepared for your overhead, although there will be a few additions and adjustments that we will cover later.

All of the expenses make up the amount of the **total expenses**. Of course, the next step is to subtract your total expenses from your total earnings. That number will tell you how much you earned during the specific time period *before* you subtract the taxes due on these earnings. That number is called "**earnings before taxes.**"

The earnings-before-taxes total is close to the amount you will report as taxable income on your tax returns. Taxes refer to federal, state, and possibly local taxes owed on this income.

We are going to use 25 percent as the rate for taxes due. The process of calculating the actual amount of taxes you owe on your income is complicated and beyond the scope of this book. Your accountant or tax preparer can give you an estimate of how much you will owe.

Once you have an estimate of the tax amount, you can subtract it from your earnings before taxes to figure out your final number, your **net income.**

"**Gross income**" is the first number we started with, the total amount collected for a given time period. "Net income" is the last number on the report. This is the amount earned after all expenses and taxes are paid.

Figure 10.1 is a copy of Becky's income statement. Her statement shows exactly how much money she collected during her first year in her new office. It also shows the amount she spent for each expense category and the taxes she anticipated paying on her earnings. Finally, it shows how much money Becky was able to put into her own account after paying the expenses and taxes on her earnings.

Figure 10.1

Becky's Income Statement
for the Year Ended December 31, 2014

```
TOTAL EARNINGS ..................................... $66,400
EXPENSES
    Rent ................................................. $12,000
    Licenses ................................................ $300
    Advertising/ marketing/website ............. $2,000
    Amortization/depreciation .................... $1,000
    Automobile expenses ............................ $2,500
    Bank and credit card fees ..................... $1,300
    Communication .................................... $2,400
    Dues ....................................................... $800
    Health insurance ................................... $3,100
    Liability insurance ................................... $200
    Renters insurance ................................... $500
    Interest ................................................ $2,000
    Legal/professional ................................ $1,200
    Meals and entertainment (business) ....... $800
    Professional development ....................... $900
    Retirement fund contribution .............. $3,000
    Supplies ................................................. $800
    Taxes (local, business) ............................ $200
    Travel (business) .................................. $1,000
TOTAL EXPENSES ................................. $36,000
NET EARNINGS BEFORE TAXES ............ $30,400
Taxes (federal and state) ........................ $5,400
NET INCOME ...................................... $25,000
```

The Income Statement's Value to You

You may still be wondering how useful the income statement is for you. After all, you're a small-business owner running a one-person operation. It may even seem like a bother and a waste of time. Not so. In fact, reviewing your income statement will help you in your business in a number of ways.

The income statement is a quick snapshot of your business that instantly provides information about your business's overall financial health and tells you, among other things, if you're making enough money to cover your overhead. If the answer is no, you can consider what options you might want to take by asking yourself the following questions:

1. What expenses could you lower to decrease expenses and thereby increase net income?
2. How much more revenue do you need to collect to pay the overhead plus have a positive net income at the bottom of the report?
3. Is it time to increase your fees?
4. What can you do to increase income?

What if the number at the bottom of the statement, the net income, is larger than you expected? That could indicate that it's time for several actions. First, you may need to meet with your accountant to discuss if you need to increase your IRS estimated tax payments. Also, it may be time to buy that new computer system you've been considering for your business. Is it time to look into hiring an assistant or an associate in your office? If you did so, how would it impact your income statement?

Comparing the most recent income statement to the one that covered the same time period during the previous year will give you yet more information. What are the differences? What are the similarities? What trends and patterns do you see? Consider what's happened in your business that's contributed to the pattern or the change in the report. For example, how much of an impact did your last marketing campaign make on your revenue? Was it worth it to pay that marketing firm to do an ad?

Tracking your money will also provide you with insight about how your website is impacting your business. If you see that adding another page to your website increased your income, how much would adding a blog or a newsletter increase your income?

In reviewing this statement, you'll see any problems that may be developing, and you'll be able to take steps to correct them before damage is done to your business. Look specifically for categories that may be costing you more than necessary. Interest expense is a good example of this. Is it time to find a lower interest rate that won't consume so much of your hard-earned revenue?

The income statement your money-software program prints out will feature percentages for each of the expense categories. Percentages are an excellent way to track the spending patterns of your business. As you become familiar with them, quickly take note of any changes in a specific category.

Some Odds and Ends to Resolve

When I assist fellow therapists with financial questions, I find they often ask about a few general issues. While these fall into a kind of "odds-and-ends" category, it's worth get-

Meet Your Income Statement

ting them out of the way by addressing them here.

One question has to do with what income should be reported. This has nothing to do with cash payments from clients—it is mandatory to report all income to the IRS, including cash payments. The question concerns balance-due accounts that clients or insurance companies have not paid by the end of the year. You don't have to report money until you actually receive the money. Once it's available for deposit into your account, it becomes income to you, and you'll need to report it in that tax period. The method of reporting income and expenses that I describe here is referred to as the "cash method." My guess is that 100 percent of mental health professionals utilize this method. The term "cash method" does not refer literally to cash. Rather, it refers to reporting actual money received and actual money spent for expenses during a specific time period.

There are certain types of businesses that use what's called the "accrual method" to report earnings. With this approach, money is counted as earnings as soon as it's due to the business. If we used the accrual method in our businesses, we would have to report the money we were waiting to receive from insurance companies and clients who didn't pay at the time of service. For our purposes, you should know that you are a cash-basis business. You will see a box on the schedule C that asks if you are cash or accrual. You will always be cash.

When I was doing tax returns for self-employed people, I was frequently asked if it was okay to deduct the time they'd donated to someone who hadn't been able to pay. The answer is always no, and I sometimes followed that answer with a comment like, "You earned bricks in heaven." If no money changed hands, there cannot be a deduction. Most of the therapists I know have a client or two who they see for little or no money. There is no expense deduction for the time spent in these sessions, but hopefully, the desire to be of service provides satisfaction for this kind action.

A similar situation arises with "bad-debt" accounts. Again, the question is whether you can write off the money a client owed you but never paid you. Once more, the answer is no. You did not receive any income for that service, so there cannot be a deduction or a write-off for that amount. As a cash-method business, you report all income received and only the deductions you actually paid.

One time when I helped a therapist-friend named Jennifer with her taxes, she asked about a situation from the previous year. A client had come for therapy a few times and had seemed pleased with the work they had done. About a month later, Jennifer was shocked when the client contacted her to say that the sessions had upset her terribly and that Jennifer must have done something dreadful during them to upset her so much. The client then demanded that Jennifer refund her the money she had paid for the sessions. Jennifer was confident that she had done a good job and had behaved in a professional, ethical, and competent manner. However, she was concerned that the woman might spread negative rumors about her. Consequently, she decided to reimburse the client and sent her the money with a note wishing her well.

Jennifer wanted to know if she could deduct the amount she had reimbursed the client. The answer in that case was yes. There was income received and income returned, which made it a deductible expense. The same principle applies when an insurance company reimburses you for work the client previously paid for. When you refund that money back to the client, it becomes a reduction of income to you, so it's deductible.

Another odds-and-ends question has to do with **amortization.** When you first start your business, expenses are typically large and may include build-out, lease-hold improvements, new furnishings, carpet, and equipment, among others things. You are not allowed to deduct all of these initial expenses in one tax year. The reason is that the expenses represent items in your business that will last a number of years, and so you "amortize" them over a period of years. A typical scenario would be that you rented an office, signed a five-year lease, and paid for a build-out to create the offices you needed. The build-out costs are divided by the number of years of the lease on the property, which in this case is five years. For the first five years you're in that office, you should deduct one-fifth of the total build-out expense. That is amortization.

Depreciation is yet another way to deduct only a portion of a large expense over a period of years. There are many rules and methods involved with depreciation. I just want you to know about the concept so that you'll be prepared with a list of all large items, their costs, and their dates of purchase when you go to your tax preparer. Such items would include computers, office equipment, furniture, and, if you use it in your business, your vehicle. Your accountant will handle the depreciation of such large items on your taxes.

The other question I get a lot has to do with credit card purchases and the interest paid on the amount due. Let's look at the first part of the question. As soon as you purchase an item for your business (assuming it's not a large purchase that will qualify for depreciation), even if it you bought it completely on credit, it goes on your expenses or purchases list. The second part of the question refers to the interest paid on the balance owed. That interest is a business expense and is entirely deductible. That's why it's a good idea to have one specific credit card that you use exclusively for business expenses.

11

HOW MUCH DO I GET TO KEEP? PROFIT-MARGIN RATIO

There is something else that Becky could calculate from her income statement: —her profit-margin ratio.

"What?" you say. Hang on. I'll show you exactly how to do this calculation and explain what information it provides you.

Profit-Margin Ratio

Becky wanted to know what percentage of all the money she actually collected was hers to keep. That's likely something you would also like to know. So let's figure it out.

Accountants tend to call the same thing by many different names with very slight, nuanced differences that make little sense to the rest of us. For example, "profit-margin ratio" is sometimes referred to as "return-on-sales ratio" or "gross-profit ratio." There's no reason for you to worry about these terms, because they actually apply to profit margins for someone like the guy down the street who owns a landscaping business and a nursery with thousands of plants and has many employees. We want to understand specifically what is important to you and your business. For our purposes, using the term "profit-margin ratio" is just fine.

In this chapter we're going to discuss the following questions, among others:
- What is the profit-margin ratio?
- Why is it good for you to know what yours is?
- How do we calculate the profit-margin ratio?
- What is the acceptable minimum ratio for a service business such as a mental health professional's business?

If you want to know the profitability of your business, you must know its profit-margin ratio. In fact, it will show you how much of every dollar you collected actually ended up in your bank account. This is a quick way to measure how much profit you're making from your business.

Calculating the profit-margin ratio is an easy division process. The income statement provides all of the numbers you need to do this calculation. The total amount of revenue, or earnings collected, is the top number on your income statement, and the last number is the amount of net income. These are the two numbers you need. Remember that net income is the final amount after you've paid expenses and taxes; thus, it is the amount that goes in your pocket. Now divide the big number (total income) into the little number (net income). This will give you a number with a decimal point. Writing that number as a percentage will show you the percentage of every dollar you collected that was yours (that is, that ended up in your bank account). Once you've calculated the profit-margin ratio of your current year, compare it to last year's.

Ideally, your profit-margin ratio should increase every year. If it's declining, you'll need to explore why. The first place to check is variable expenses. Look for significant

How Much Do I Get to Keep? Profit-Margin Ratio

changes in any of those categories. The other place to look is total income; compare your current total income number with that of a prior period of time to see how it's changed. If the total income has decreased, figure out why that is, or at least surmise why that would be the case.

Most industries have profit-margin ratios that apply specifically to their particular industry. In a service industry such as mental health, professionals expect to earn a profit of at least 30 percent of every dollar collected; such a profit margin shows that the business is stable. If you go to the bank for a loan and have a 30 percent profit-margin ratio, the banker will know that your business will likely repay the loan.

Another important piece of information you can gather from your profit-margin ratio concerns your pricing strategies. Pricing the product is a critical part of any business plan. You want a fee that provides you with a minimum of a 30 percent profit, supplies you with the number of clients necessary to keep your schedule sufficiently full, and reflects the value of the service you provide.

Because the question of your fee is so important, I am going to address it more completely in chapter 15. There, we will cover the complex questions that professional mental health workers frequently discuss and worry about. What is the right fee to charge? How and when should the fee be raised? Is it better to work more for less or to work less for more? There are many issues surrounding this fee question. We will leave it here for now but pick it up again in more detail later.

What if your ratio is below 30 percent? I mentioned earlier in this chapter the need to review expenses, particularly variable ones, to see where you can cut back. When doing an analysis of your pricing strategy, you may discover that you need to increase your fee. Charging just ten dollars more per session can have a big impact on your total earnings number. Play with these numbers and see what it would take you to get your profit-margin ratio up over 30 percent.

As an example, let's calculate Becky's profit ratio. Look back at Becky's income statement in Figure 10.1. Her total earnings amount is $66,400. Her net income (income after all expenses, including federal taxes, are paid) is $25,000. Now use the following formula:

$$\text{Profit-Margin Ratio} = \frac{\text{Net Income}}{\text{Total Earnings}}$$

$$\frac{\text{Becky's Net Income (\$25,000)}}{\text{Becky's Total Income (\$66,400)}} = \text{Becky's Profit-Margin Ratio (37.65 percent)}$$

Divide the big number into the little number to get Becky's profit-margin ratio, and the result is 37.65 percent. Becky is above the minimum industry profit-margin ratio of 30 percent. During her first year in private practice, she kept her income and expenses in balance. Now imagine that Becky has plans for her second year to expand her website, which will increase her expenses. If her income increases proportionally, income to expenses, she will likely stay above 30 percent.

That gives us enough information to easily examine Becky's (and your) break-even point. Let's discuss that now.

12

JUST ENOUGH: BREAK-EVEN POINT

We will now tackle the next logical question after completing the calculations to determine overhead and the profit-margin ratio. The answer to this question will show you how many paid session hours you need to do to cover your overhead, which, in business language, is your **break-even point**.

It is possible at this point to use a lot of accounting terminology, graphs, and even algebra. Fortunately, there is no reason for so much complexity. An accountant-friend might wonder why we aren't going into more detail and specifics on how to calculate the break-even point. The answer is that you don't need all that other stuff. Tell them that.

Onward.

The term "break-even point" refers to how many "**units**" the owner needs to sell to cover the overhead. A unit could be a car, a shirt, or a gallon of milk. Anything that is being sold can be referred to as a unit.

The business model we use is time for money. We sell our time and our expertise and organize our time into sessions. Most therapists do sessions that are about one hour long. In business language, then, the unit we sell is a session, or an hour. When we speak about "**unit volume**," we are referring to the number of sessions or hours done in a specific time frame.

Then the question becomes the following: how many sessions/hours does your business have to sell to cover your overhead? One could also ask, "What is your break-even unit volume in sessions/hours?"

Of course, you're probably already ahead of me on this next question. The number of sessions required to cover the overhead is dependent upon the price per unit.

What is the fee you charge and collect for a session? Is it always the same fee, or is there a range? When we contract with insurance companies, we agree to accept their fee. Due to the many variables that determine insurance company fee schedules or reimbursements, it is almost impossible to state only one number as the amount paid for a session. Therefore, the best way to approach this question is to calculate the average amount you collect per session over a given period of time. I know you know how to do this, but I'll offer just a quick note here to refresh your math memory. To calculate the average, add up the amount collected over a specific period of time. Next add up the number of sessions you did in that same time period. Divide the amount of money collected by the number of sessions you did, and you'll have the average amount per session.

For our example, we will stay with Becky's number that we discussed in a previous chapter. Consider the following:
- Becky's overhead was $36,000 per year.
- To get Becky's average session fee, take her total income earned ($66,400) divided by the total number of sessions (unit volume) done for the year. Becky did 920 sessions.

Just Enough: Break-Even Point

Total earnings ÷ number of sessions =
average fee per session
$66,400 ÷ 920 = $70 average fee per session

- How many sessions does Becky have to do to cover her overhead of $36,000—that is, to achieve her break-even point? Divide the overhead amount of $36,000 by her average fee per session of $70.
  Annual overhead ÷ average session fee =
  break-even unit volume
  $36,000 ÷ $70 = 514 sessions

- Of the 920 sessions Becky does that year, 514 go toward overhead.

If Becky does 20 sessions a week for 25 weeks, she will cover her overhead for the year and be at her break-even point. That means that she'll be working the first half of the year to cover her overhead. Well, that feels a bit depressing. What is another way to look at this that puts some money in her pocket during the first 25 weeks?

Let's do the same calculations, but instead of looking at an annual break-even point, we'll look at Becky's (and your) monthly break-even point:

- Becky's annual overhead is $36,000. Figure her monthly overhead average is $3,000.
- We know her average fee per session is $70.
- Now, on a monthly basis, how many sessions will Becky have to do for the month to hit her break-even point?

$3,000 ÷ $70 = 43 break-even unit volume in sessions

- Becky knows that the first 43 sessions of the month are going toward overhead and toward meeting her break-even point.

If you want to break that down even more to a weekly break-even point, it's easy to do. Use an average of 4 weeks per month, and divide the monthly break-even session (Becky's was 43) number by 4, and you'll have a weekly break-even number. Becky's calculation shows that she will start making a profit after she does 11 sessions during the week. On a busy week, that could mean Becky will hit her break-even point on Wednesday.

Let's now go back to the two ways that Becky and you can get to the break-even point more quickly. Once again, these are by increasing your fee or lowering your overhead. Yet another way is to increase the number of sessions you do during a given time period, which obviously makes for a greater profit.

It is important to know what your break-even unit volume is. As discussed previously, even a small increase in income or a decrease in expenses can have a positive impact on your break-even point, which is when you can start putting money in your pocket.

All Months Are Not Created Equal

When you look over your monthly income statements for the past few years, you'll quickly see a pattern emerge. Some months are just not as busy or as profitable as others. December, the peak of the holiday season, is when clients are much less likely to schedule appointments. Summer vacation schedules may also interfere with the rhythm of your business.

Professionals know and anticipate the change in the volume of business during these slower months. These times are the ideal times to take your vacation or to attend seminars and training conferences to complete your CEUs.

But you still need to pay the overhead in the slow months. Once you've been profitable enough to build up your business savings account such that it can cover overhead for a minimum of three months, you won't need to worry. But until then, you'll need to know how to take into account the weeks or months when your revenue decreases.

Since there are months in which you may not be able to hit your break-even point, it helps to look at the numbers for the entire year. Review your annual earnings and expenses to see if, over a period of time, you will be able to cover your expenses. As an example, let's look at the month of December. The last two weeks of the year are usually very slow, and you can't expect to earn much revenue during that time. If you know you need $2,000 per week to cover overhead, anticipate that cost by saving enough during the year to pay December and early January expenses. Most therapists can count on business picking up again after the first of the year.

An Extra Note about the Break-Even Point

In addition to being useful when discussing annual overhead and expense figures, the term "break-even point" is also important when you're planning a specific project. For example, say you and your office mates decide to present a training for other professionals. To do so, you need to determine what the costs involved are going to be. Once you decide on a fair price to charge for your event, you can find out how many people you'll need to sign up to reach your break-even point by dividing the total cost by the fee you're charging. If you reach the break-even number of attendees, all of your expenses will be covered. If you sign up more than that number, you will have a profit; if you sign up fewer attendees than the break-even number, you and your office mates will have to absorb some of the costs of the event.

A Short Clock Review

These last seven chapters are filled with a lot of information. Let's take a quick look at the highlights we've covered. It will be a great help to review these as you become more involved with organizing and tracking your business finances.

The following is a list of what we've covered thus far:
- five things you need to know to set up a private practice
- three things that will be very useful in your business
- the one thing that will help you sleep better at night
- your business overhead and how to determine it
- what an income statement is and how it is useful to you
- why "profit-margin ratio" means the break-even point and how to calculate it.

Now it is time to take a close look at your cash flow.

13

CHECK YOUR GAS GAUGE: CASH FLOW

Cash—the money in your bank account—is what makes your business possible. Gasoline is a good metaphor for cash. Your car runs just fine as long as there's gas in it. Run out of gas, and the whole thing stops. It's the same with cash and your business.

Your earnings number may look really strong, but that doesn't necessarily mean your cash flow is as healthy. There are some situations that can trigger low cash supplies. By being aware of what they are, you'll be better equipped to not let them derail you.

First, though, let's take a look at the **cash-flow statement**, the second very important financial statement we'll discuss in this book.

What is the Cash-Flow Statement?

The cash-flow statement looks very similar to your business checking account's statement. It is straightforward, easy to read, and loaded with information. As a rule, you can run these statements on a monthly or weekly basis. We'll look at a monthly statement.

The first line on the cash-flow statement is called "**beginning cash.**" This is the amount of cash that was left over at the end of the previous month. The next line shows **cash in.** This is the money that showed up in your bank account during a particular time period (e.g., a month or a week). The next line, named "**cash out,**" is the total of the cash that came out of your business for that time period. Finally, after adding the cash in and subtracting the cash out, you have the **ending cash.**

By now, I hope you have a good idea of what it costs to run your business every month—that is, its overhead. For most months, the amount of cash out will be close to your expected usual amount. The months that you have expenses due that are not typical can cause a cash-flow problem. For example, annual payments due for insurance and professional organizations, travel for CEUs, and estimated tax payments are among the cash outlays that can create a tight cash flow.

Sample of a Cash-Flow Statement

Quicken (or your money-management software program) will run a cash-flow statement for you. Here's a simple example of what that kind of statement could look like:

<u>**September Cash-Flow Statement**</u>
Beginning cash	$3,000
Cash in	$8,000
Cash out	($9,000)
Ending cash	$2,000

It is helpful to do a quick cash-flow budget for each month based on a review of your past year's monthly cash flows. That will help you plan carefully for the next twelve months. A list of monthly expected expenses broken down into a week's-due sheet is included in the appendix and on our website. I find that this form is helpful in planning cash-flow needs and in spreading the expenses out through the month.

Does Cash Equal Income?

It's important to remember that cash and income are not always the same. Your net-income statement shows what your earnings were over a specific period of time—for example, over a month or a quarter. However, the net-income statement doesn't say anything about your cash balance.

A major cash-flow drain for self-employed people is the process of taking money from their business account for personal expenses. The money you take out is your "draw," which is something that the income statement doesn't include. While the income statement may show that you have a net income of $4,000 for the month, if you have withdrawn $4,500 from the account, you could be at risk for overdrawing your business checking account. That's why it's especially helpful for you (or your software) to run a cash-flow statement every week.

Along with the personal withdrawals from your account, there are other situations that can create cash-flow problems.

You probably accept credit card payment for services. As you know, it generally takes about two business days for the money to show up in your bank account. Your earnings will reflect that money, but you can't consider it cash until it's in the bank.

Credit card companies also charge a fee that comes out

of your bank account, usually at the beginning of the following month. Even if you deposited $7,000 in credit card payments that month, that fee will decrease between 2 percent and as much as 6 percent when the credit card company removes the fee from your account. Remember, then, not to think of all of the money in your account as cash without subtracting the credit card fee first.

As we all know too well, insurance reimbursements can be painfully slow. Initial claims submitted usually take significantly longer to process and to pay than ongoing claims. All insurance companies seem to slow down in January, even though the claims were filed on the previous year's benefits. Consequently, it is never wise to count on insurance checks to help with cash flow for the month of January.

Did you or your biller forget about sending in the insurance claim? You may be counting on incoming revenue from an insurance company only to find out that the claim is still on your desk. Bounced client checks are another ongoing problem; until checks are covered, the cash isn't there. Clients' failures to pay their bills can be another dent in your cash flow. (That is why I always advise collecting at the time of the services rendered.)

You can plan ahead for the months your insurances and estimated taxes are due, but sometimes situations crop up that require payment for things not in the budget. In our office we had the unhappy occurrence of water leaking through our floor to the ceiling of the office below. We were responsible for the repairs to that office's damages. Nowhere in our budget could you find a "toilet-runs-over" expense. (But we did buy a heavy-duty plunger and offer plunging lessons to everyone in the office.)

Have you ever gone shopping at Costco or Sam's Club

and overspent because eventually you're going to need all of that stuff only to realize later in the week that you don't have enough cash to pay for milk and bread? The same thing can happen in your business. A new computer, for example, is a major expense. To keep your budget intact, set aside money ahead of time so that you don't end up having to pay for major expenses out of current earnings. Current earnings are for current, budgeted, and planned-for-expenses.

There's yet another factor to consider when thinking about payment for major expenses: When you pay in full at the time of the purchase, such as for a new computer, your bank statement will show withdrawal of the complete amount. Your net income-statement, however, may list it only as a percentage of the expense. That's because of depreciation. (See chapter 10.) Computers are items that last more than a year, and your income statement notes only the percentage based on depreciation for that one year, not on the entire expense.

The timing of payments is important when considering cash flow. If you're paying the current month's bills with last month's earnings, feel free to pay as the bills come in. When you have to rely on current income, it's smart to spread payments out over the month rather than deplete your cash early in the month. It's important to always have some cash available.

Cash is always king. You cannot run a business without cash. Keep a close eye on your cash flow, and if you see that your cash is getting lean, figure out ways to correct the situation. Do you have outstanding receivables you can pursue, payments you can delay, or spending you can curtail? Do what you must to fatten up your cash stores.

14

STAYING ON TRACK: BANK RECONCILIATION

Now that we're on the subject of cash and checking accounts, it's a good time to explain how to do a bank reconciliation and why you need to do one every month. Money-management software makes it simple; doing it by your checkbook is much more work. The principles are the same: you're confirming that your records and the bank's agree on how much money went into your account and how much came out. Typically, the closing balance on your bank statement is different from the closing balance on your check ledger for the corresponding date. The purpose of a bank reconciliation is to ensure that this difference can be explained and verified.

Gather together the items you need: your check ledger, either kept by hand or on your software program, and the bank statement that corresponds with the dates on your ledger.

Next compare each transaction on your bank statement with your check ledger. It is easiest to do this comparison by category. For example, compare each deposit listed in your ledger with each deposit listed on your bank statement, and then go on to checks and withdrawals. Place a check mark near each item on both the ledger and the bank records after you've confirmed that they're exactly the same. If you find you made a mistake when you entered an amount into your check ledger, correct that now. Your computer will do the math for you, or you can do it with a calculator.

On your check ledger, you will probably have checks that have not yet cleared your bank, which are referred to as "checks outstanding." If you're doing this process by hand, write out a list of the outstanding checks and total them.

If you have deposits on your check ledger that are not on the bank statement, make a list of them. It's unusual to have deposits like that since most of us make deposits during bank hours. Any deposits that don't make it onto the bank statement are considered a "deposit in transit."

The next step is to adjust the balance on the bank statement to the true, adjusted, or corrected balance. This corrected balance refers to the balance that's on your check ledger. This is the actual amount of money in your account, not the amount shown as the closing balance on your bank statement. To do that, make the following adjustments to the bank statement closing balance:

    Add: Deposits in transit
    Deduct: Outstanding checks

You now have an **adjusted statement balance** that reflects the actual amount in your bank for that date. If you have done this correctly, the adjusted statement balance will be the exact amount you have in your bank ledger.

To confirm that your checkbook balance is correct, start with your check ledger's month-end balance and follow these steps:

Add: Any items from the bank statement not entered onto your ledger
Deduct: Any charges not entered onto your ledger

This is the **adjusted check ledger balance.** Both of the two adjusted balances must be the same amount. Even if you are off by just a few pennies, it is worth taking the time to find your mistake to be certain that you have the correct amount of cash in your account.

A little trick that all accountants and bookkeepers know is that if the adjusted statement and ledger numbers are different by any number divisible by nine, you've probably inverted a number in one of your checkbook entries. That means you could have entered $72 instead of the correct number, $27. The difference is $45, a number divisible by nine. Just a little helpful hint.

Regular bank reconciliations assure that you have an accurate idea of the cash in your bank account, thereby preventing checks from coming back as NSF (nonsufficient funds), which is both expensive and embarrassing. If you have an employee who manages the bank account, signs the checks, and keeps the records, as a way to prevent fraud, have someone else do the actual bank reconciliation.

15

STRUGGLES WITH FEES: SETTING THE RIGHT FEES

For many mental health professionals, setting and relaying fees is fraught with discomfort. Becky said that when potential clients asked her on the phone about her fee, she would be almost apologetic when she answered. Likewise, when it's time to ask the client for payment, Becky said her nerves kicked in. She added that she would love to have a front-desk person handle all money transactions, thus keeping her out of the finance loop.

What a dilemma. Our business is to provide a service to clients and to provide money for ourselves. It's almost ironic that as therapists, we're comfortable discussing the most personal aspects of our clients' lives, but many of us squirm when we must discuss fees.

Let's step away a bit to get some perspective about the best practices for handling fee matters.

Know the Fee Range in Your Area

Businesses shop around to know what their competitors charge, and you need to do the same. What are the going rates for therapy in your specific geographic and demographic area? Keep in mind there are always outliers on both ends of the scale. At the low end, interns who need to fulfill their licensing hours are willing to work for meager rates, and agencies set up to receive grants and charitable funds can offer services with sliding-fee schedules.

You, though, want to find out the rates of therapists who attract people in your target market and have an amount of experience similar to yours. Your goal in setting the right fee is to be competitive *and* profitable. Once you've gained experience and expertise, especially in particular areas, you can tilt your fees higher than many other therapists in your area. Clients are willing to pay more when they know that they're receiving excellent therapy.

To find out what the going rates are, have a friend or a family member call to request information about another therapist's fees and appointment availability. Or if you have friends in the business, you could comfortably inquire about their fee structures. This is not to suggest that professionals get together and agree to charge a certain fee. It is simply to inform yourself of the going rates in your area and to decide on an amount that you feel your services are worth.

Know Your Profit-Margin Ratio

When you used the formula to calculate your profit-margin ratio, was your percentage over or under 30 percent? Remember that 30 percent represents only the minimal acceptable profit ratio for the health care industry and that many factors can influence this percentage.

If you live in a more expensive area, both your business and personal expenses will be higher. In that case, you may find that you need a profit ratio of 35 or 45 percent. If your profit ratio keeps you competitive and you're able to maintain a full schedule, having a higher ratio may be exactly right for you.

Other factors also impact profit ratios. For example, you may want to pursue extra education that will help you grow your business and develop your expertise. Additional education can be both expensive and time consuming, and during that period of time, your profit-margin ratio may well go down because you'll have higher expenses and a lower work volume. However, once you complete the education and bring what you've learned into full action, you'll be able to market yourself as the preferred clinician in town to treat a particular type of client or issue. And with that education, there's a good chance you'll see your profit ratio go well above 30 percent.

We see, then, there are outliers in the higher and lower range of fees, but there is also a substantial middle range. Those just starting out need time to develop the expertise required to handle difficult and challenging cases and are not comfortable setting higher fees. I frequently see how grateful new therapists in our group are to have every session that comes their way. We were all there once.

Roger, for example, came to us newly licensed and straight out of graduate school. He set a low fee and booked as many clients as he possibly could. When we calculated his profit-margin ratio, it was only 20 percent. But he was fine with that. He said that he had planned carefully for the years that it would take to build his business. During that period, he didn't feel he had enough expertise to be worth more than what he was charging.

After Roger had been in our office for about two years, he told me that he was amazed by how much he'd learned and grown in his profession. With a higher confidence level and better skills as a therapist, he was ready to increase his fees. Roger was careful about how he increased them, gradually bringing fees up over the next year. He was also careful to keep his overhead low, which allowed the increased fees to go directly into his profit.

Understanding Profit

The decision to raise your fee concerns not only what the going rate in your area is, but also how full your appointment schedule is. Are most of your appointments filled? Do you have a waiting list of people who want to see you? Are you turning people away? Are you booking too many sessions each week because you don't like to turn anyone away?

These are all questions you'll need to answer when considering if it's the right time to raise your rate. Most clinicians prefer a workload of between twenty and twenty-five sessions a week because booking more than that is too exhausting. The industry average, as previously mentioned, is twenty sessions per week.

Analyze Your Fee Structure

You now have a lot of business information at your disposal that can help you determine the correct fee for your services. You know your overhead, your break-even point, your cash flow, and, very importantly, your profit-margin ratio. You also are aware of the population and demographic your business attracts. Of course, you don't want to price yourself out of your market, but use all of this information to examine whether you can slightly increase your fee. Assume, for a moment, that you do about one thousand sessions a year. A $10 increase would boost your profit by $10,000, assuming you didn't use the additional funds to increase expenses as well. (I know I'm starting to sound repetitive on that point, but we all tend to spend more than we earn. Keep overhead low.)

Many mental health professionals tell me that they experience a lot of discomfort when they answer the question, "What do you charge?" A way to answer that question that helps the professional feel more comfortable is to avoid using the first person. Instead of responding, "I charge fifty dollars," say instead, "The fee for that service is fifty dollars."

But underneath the clinician's discomfort is the personal values question the professional may have about his or her own services. (I just felt storm clouds rolling in.) The professional may wonder if he or she is worth that amount of money. As a result of feeling undeserving of money or insecure about the amount to charge, many professionals keep their fee structures lower than necessary, causing them to schedule more sessions per day just to cover overhead and make a profit. We all know of clinicians who will do ten sessions a day rather than raise their fee.

One way to analyze your fee is to calculate how much you would make at your current rate if you did between 20 and 25 sessions per week. For example, if you only charge $50 per session, multiply that rate by 25 ($50 × 25 sessions = $1,250 earnings per week).

But you know that $1,250 per week will not cover your overhead and provide you with a profit. We'll assume that you calculated your overhead and needed profit and that you know you must earn at least $2,250 per week. To solve this problem, you decide to work harder and longer and to schedule more sessions. After you do the calculations, you figure that you can schedule 45 sessions per week and that

that will provide you with sufficient earnings ($50 × 45 sessions = $2,250).

It won't take you or any other clinician very long to become exhausted working at the rate of 45 sessions per week. What would be a reasonable fee that could cover expenses and provide a profit and not leave you feeling as though you're working two full-time jobs? When we divide the cost plus the profit total needed, which is $2,250, by the industry standard of 25, we get a fee of $90 ($2,250 ÷ 25 = $90).

This increase may feel too big to do all at one time. In that case, introduce it in $20 increments over a period of six to eight months.

Remember that when analyzing your fee structure, your goal is to schedule 20 to 25 sessions per week, earn sufficient revenue to pay all of your expenses, and have a profit margin that is above the minimal profit margin of 30 percent. Charge a fee that is fair and honors the value of the work you do.

Times to Collect Fees

There is no ironclad rule about the best time to collect fees from your clients. Some clinicians like to take care of it at the beginning of the session. They explain their policy to the client during the initial session so that the client is prepared. Other therapists collect payment at the end of the session. That gives them flexibility should they want to offer their client a longer session than was scheduled. In those cases, it's important to make it clear to the client that accepting the offer of additional time involves an additional fee.

Many clinicians and clients prefer to keep a credit card on file with the clinician. That allows the clinician to input the credit card information at the end of the day without taking any time away from sessions to do payments.

As I have stressed in prior chapters, whichever timing you prefer, it is crucial to collect fees at the time of service. Whether your client pays a co-pay for insurance or pays cash out of pocket, collect it that day. It is never a good idea to let your receivables (uncollected revenue) accumulate.

How to Ask for Money

If you collect payment at the beginning of sessions, you probably explained that procedure to your clients beforehand. That means that they generally come prepared to hand you a check, a credit card, or cash. You can make a comment such as, "Let's get the business stuff out of the way so that we can focus on your session" to remind clients to take care of payment before you start. Do not sit back in your therapist role until you've handled this.

If you collect payment at the end of your sessions, take your body out of therapist mode. You might sit forward in your chair, stand up, walk over to your desk, or go to your scheduling device. Any of these movements will inform your client that you're moving into the business of establishing the next appointment and taking care of payment. You can easily ask the client, "How would you like to take care of today's session—credit card, check, or cash?" Memorize this simple question. After you've practiced it a few times, you'll find that it just rolls off your tongue easily and comfortably.

There are professionals whose reluctance to or discomfort around setting and collecting fees ends up costing them thousands of dollars each year. I have known clinicians who collect only the money insurance companies pay them in order to avoid having to ask clients for it. Feel good about the work you're doing, and keep in mind that you should always value your time and expertise. You are providing clients with the service they want. The fees you receive from them demonstrate the value of that.

16

BE PREPARED: TAX WISDOM

There are so many tax pitfalls for the self-employed business owner that it's hard to know where to begin. I've decided to start with a story.

It was a lovely summer day, and my son and his family had come to visit us. The kids and I were having a great time in the pool, playing one water game after another. My husband came outside with the mail and announced that we had received a letter from the IRS. No one ever wants to get a letter from those folks. I jumped out of the pool, read the letter, and sighed, knowing that I had a lot of work ahead of me. Our tax return had been randomly selected for a "line-item audit" based on the fact that I'm self-employed. That's the kind of audit that requires substantiation for *every* item, *every* line, and *every* number on the entire tax return. *Yuck!*

The next workday I phoned the IRS agent assigned to our audit. She explained that she would be coming either to our home or to my office to do the audit and asked how long it would take me to prepare for our first meeting. I anticipated that it'd take about three months and opted for the house, where I transfer all my business files. We set the date and scheduled the first of her many appointments. Thus began the summer we would term "the summer of the audit."

In the thirteen years I was in tax preparation and accounting, I worked directly with many doctors and staff in health care providers' offices. I prepared their monthly profit-and-loss statements and their taxes. After passing the IRS Special Enrollment Examination, I became a certified IRS enrolled agent, eligible to represent clients in a tax audit. But this was different. This was *my* tax audit—a line-item tax audit.

So I got busy. I spent every weekend organizing documents, copying receipts, and putting them in files. In each file I placed a top sheet that listed every item making up the total amount for that line so that the auditor could clearly see what expense or income each particular line included. I labeled each file with the corresponding form name and line on our tax return. Every form on the return had a spot on the couch in my office. Under each label was the stack of files that supported the lines on that form. I was ready.

The auditor and I spent many hours together. I was pleased when she told me that the other auditors in her office were jealous of how well prepared I was. She also explained to me that we'd been randomly selected because the IRS was doing a study on the ways that sole proprietors could cheat on their tax returns. I laughingly replied that I could certainly fill them in on that. I have prepared hundreds of self-employed individuals' tax returns and have always been astonished by how cavalier many tax filers are with the information and paperwork they need to substantiate information on their schedule C, the sole-proprietor tax form.

Due to delays, the audit took almost a year to complete, but at the end of it, the final report noted that the IRS owed us an additional $400. It was a lost summer, but you can imagine how grateful I was for the files, receipts, and financial records I had kept and for the good accounting principles I had used in running my business.

I share this story because the reality is that you too could receive a letter requesting the same careful review of your business. The need to maintain good records is paramount. Every item you deduct on your tax return must have a credit card statement and preferably a receipt verifying its credibility. My filing procedure is to set up a file for each month and to place the supporting document in the appropriate month's file. For the audit, I had to go through and reorganize the documents into subject/topics to correspond with the lines on my schedule C.

Income reporting is very strict. Overstating expenses results in paying the IRS more money. But understating income is a felony for which people can go to jail. Fortunately, my biller/bookkeeper does a year-end summary that lists every client I've seen that year and the amount paid on each account. For the auditor, I whited out clients' names and gave her the summary statement, which immediately validated the accuracy of my total earnings reported on my schedule C. Bank deposits do not equal earnings. Neither does the total from the 1099s sent from insurance companies and credit card companies. You need a system that calculates the total earnings for each month and then generates an annual report at the end of each year.

Getting It Together for Your Tax-Preparer Meeting

Your tax preparer/accountant needs specific items to prepare your business tax forms. If you have money software, this is easy. It categorizes each expense, and all you have to do is print out a year-end statement. However, you must separate and categorize your credit card payments when you enter the total payment into your computer; otherwise, you'll need copies of your business credit card statements. You may recall that when we discussed depreciation, I advised you to prepare a list of large items purchased for business during the tax year. Include the receipt and the date purchased. Your tax person will know what to do with these items.

If you use your vehicle for business, you can deduct auto expenses, but you must have a written log of business miles driven during that year. Driving to professional meetings, to home visits, and to shop for business items are all considered using your auto for business. Keep track of your mileage—both the total miles driven for the year and the miles driven for business. The miles you drive from your home to the office are not considered business travel, but there's an interesting twist to that rule. If one day you did a session from your home before you left for the office, the mileage to the office is deductible. This is important for the many therapists today who do sessions via the Internet or the phone from their home before heading to the office.

The percentage of auto expenses allowed depends on how many miles you drive for business compared to other miles driven. Again, divide the big number (total miles driven) into the little number (business miles driven.) If the car was used for business more than 50 percent of the time, the tax deduction will be more advantageous. If you purchased a new car during the tax year, include a copy of the sales agreement and the cost of registering your vehicle, your auto insurance, gasoline, oil changes, maintenance, car washes, parking in any garage, and interest on the loan or the lease payments.

Preparing Yourself for How Much Tax You Will Pay

The bottom number on your schedule C is the taxable income of your business. It will not look exactly like the net income you calculated on your income statement because the schedule C makes adjustments to some of the entries on the net-income statement. For example, the deduction for meals and entertainment is adjusted to allow for only 50 percent of the expense. Furthermore, other items reported on your income statement are listed on separate 1040 forms.

Two items that are not on your schedule C are on your income statement. They are the contribution you made to your pension plan and your payments for health insurance premiums. As a self-employed individual, you are eligible to take health insurance expenses as an adjustment instead of as a part of the medical deduction on a schedule A (the itemized deduction schedule).

The net income from the schedule C form is immediately subject to a 15 percent self-employment tax. Since you don't have an employer, you don't pay into social security through FICA deductions on a paycheck. Self-employed individuals must pay their own contribution to FICA, social security, and Medicare. To make that less onerous for the self-employed, the IRS allows an adjustment for half of the self-employment tax on your tax return.

Estimated tax payments, referred to as "quarterly tax payments," go to the US Treasury four times a year. Because you don't have any tax withheld on your income, you need to take this on yourself through payments on your anticipated taxable income. These are due on April 15, June 15, September 15, and January 15. Failure to pay them during the year results in a penalty that's added to the amount due when you file your return.

It is tempting for self-employed people to put off sending their estimated taxes to the IRS in a timely manner. The unfortunate result, in addition to a penalty, is that there isn't sufficient money paid ahead of the filing date to cover the taxes owed. Even if you find yourself unable to cover the complete tax bill upon filing, send in your tax return when it's due. The penalties for a failure to file are much higher than those for a failure to pay the tax due. Of course, it's better in every way to stay up to date with your taxes and to avoid the hassles of delinquent payments.

If for any reason you experience a significant change in earnings or expenses during the year, it is wise to call your tax preparer/accountant to discuss your situation. You may need to make changes to the amount you pay for estimated taxes.

Tick-tock. Yes, taxes are another one of the "clock" items that require careful attention. If you have established systems that keep your records and financial material in an orderly, well-organized manner, you'll avoid much of the hassle of tax preparation. And if you do receive an audit letter from the IRS, you'll know that every one of your organized systems is about to pay off.

17

WHAT IS YOUR BUSINESS WORTH? MEET YOUR BALANCE SHEET

You have now been introduced to and have become friendly with most of the main characters in your savvy-business-money book. Each number-character plays off the previous number-character. You can see how they intertwine, mix, play nice together, or fight with one another.

Now we are about to explore the grand finale of business money statements. This rigidly structured statement pulls together all of the other numbers and presents a clear, concise picture of your business and its viability.

The Balance Sheet

When you read the word "balance," perhaps you picture things that balance other things, like a scale used to weigh gold in the 1800s or the scales of justice. The significance of the balance sheet is that it has two distinct sides to it: a left side and a right side. Specific information and their dollar amounts go on either one side or the other. The two sides must always have equal total dollar amounts—they must balance.

Assets

Your business owns stuff. Maybe it owns just a couch, a chair, a desk, and a computer. Perhaps you bought your office building, and you have a big mortgage on it. Whatever your business owns, even if you're still paying it off, is called an asset.

Your list of assets goes on the left side of the balance sheet. They are lumped together in specific categories, in a specific order, and in the order of their liquidity. "**Liquidity**" refers to the speed with which you can turn an asset into cash. Any asset, including cash, that can be turned into cash within the next twelve months is considered "current." Cash will always be the first asset listed under **current assets**. The list of current assets will look something like this:

    Current Assets
    Cash $75,000

Current assets are followed by **fixed assets**. Fixed assets are such items as office equipment, office furnishings, and vehicles purchased and used in your business. The dollar amount for these items is the purchase price at the time of purchase. The first items lumped together under fixed assets are the smaller ones—again, they're items that could be sold or liquidated more quickly. That office building you purchased in 1995 for $90,000 is listed as a long-term asset since it will be difficult to liquidate within twelve months. It will typically be the last item listed under "fixed assets."

As you may recall, when we talked about expenses, we covered depreciation, which is the process of writing off a portion of the original cost of an asset each year. The total amount you wrote off over the years you owned the asset is listed as a subtraction from the original cost of the items. The asset side—the left side of the balance sheet—will look like this:

Current Assets	
Cash	$75,000
Fixed Assets	$35,000
Less cumulative depreciation	($20,000)
Long-Term Asset	$90,000
Less cumulative depreciation	($60,000)
Total Assets	<u>$120,000</u>

Add the dollar amounts listed to arrive at the total-assets amount. For our example here, we would add the cash and the fixed assets less the cumulative depreciation to arrive at the total-assets amount of $120,000.

Liabilities

Liabilities include the money you still owe on the stuff (the assets) you purchased for your business. If you have a bank loan, credit card debt, or a mortgage on the office building you bought, those costs will be listed on the right side of the balance sheet under **liabilities.**

Just as with assets, liabilities are listed in order of current liabilities, such as a credit card debt or a short-term note, and long-term liabilities, such as a mortgage on an office building. The amounts shown on the balance sheet are what you currently owe on these accounts.

Liabilities are added together to show the amount for **total liabilities**. This is what the items on the right side of the balance sheet will look like:

Current Liabilities
    Short-term debts $20,000
Long-Term Liabilities
    Mortgages $80,000
Total Liabilities: **$100,000**

The two sides of the statement have to be equal. They have to balance. But they don't—not yet. So enter the owner's equity account.

Owner's Equity Account

The **owner's equity account** is entered on the left side of the balance sheet under "total liabilities." This figure represents how much equity you, the business owner, have in your business at the time of this balance sheet. Use this quick formula to calculate its amount:

$$\text{Assets} - \text{liabilities} = \text{owner's equity}$$

In the example we've been using in our discussion, we'd plug the numbers into the formula as follows:

$$\$120{,}000 - \$100{,}000 = \$20{,}000$$
(owner's equity account)

Hooray! The balance sheet is now balanced. The left side and the right side both total $120,000. See the completed balance sheet in Figure 17.1

Figure 17.1

Balance Sheet

Assets		Liabilities	
Current Assets		**Current Liabilities**	
Cash	$75,000	Short-term debts	$20,000
Fixed Assets	$35,000		
Less cumulative depreciation	($20,000)		
Long-Term Assets	90,000	**Long-Term Liabilities**	
Less cumulative depreciation	($60,000)	Mortgages	$80,000
Total Assets:	**$120,000**	**Total Liabilities:**	**$100,000**
		Owner's Equity	
		Retained Earnings	$20,000
		Total Liabilities and Owner's Equity:	**$120,000**

Next we'll put some numbers on our balance sheets to get a better understanding of how these numbers work together to provide us with valuable information about this business.

Figure 17.2

Balance Sheet

Assets		Liabilities	
Current Assets	$90,000	Current Liabilities	$1,000
Fixed Assets	$35,000	Long-Term Liabilities	19,000
Less cumulative depreciation	($15,000)		
Total Assets	**$110,000**	**Total Liabilities**	**$20,000**
		Owner's Equity	
		Retained Earnings	$90,000
		Total Liabilities and Owner's Equity	**$110,000**

A balance of $90,000 cash in current assets and just $20,000 in liabilities tells us that this business's balance sheet is in good condition. There is sufficient working capital since little of the cash is used to pay large amounts toward liabilities. This business has a reasonable expectation of sustainability. Now let's look at a different scenario.

Figure 17.3
Balance Sheet

Assets		Liabilities	
Current Assets	$4,000	Current Liabilities	$8,000
Fixed Assets	$6,000	Long-Term Liabilities	$7,000
Less cumulative depreciation	($2,000)		
Total Assets	**$8,000**	**Total Liabilities**	**$15,000**
		Owner's Equity	**($7,000)**
		Total Liabilities and Owner's Equity	**$8,000**

The balance sheet shown in Figure 17.3 tells us immediately that this business is not financially sound. With cash reserves of just $4,000, the business has little liquidity. The lack of cash in current assets tells us that this business has little, if any, working capital. The only fixed asset is the computer system the owner purchased. The owner has been using credit cards to cover expenses, resulting in an increase in liabilities and a decrease in owner's equity. The current liabilities show the amount owed on credit card debt to be paid within the next twelve months. The long-term liabilities, which are the sum of long-term notes payable and the balance of the credit card owed past the current twelve-months amount, total $7,000. The lack of assets and the large amount of total liabilities result in an owner equity with a negative balance of $15,000, as shown here:

$$\text{Assets - Liabilities = Owners Equity}$$
$$\$8,000 - \$15,000 = -\$7,000$$

This business is in trouble. If something doesn't drastically change, it will be shut down or in bankruptcy. To explore why and how this business came to be in so much financial trouble, we would need to examine the income statement and the cash-flow statement. What is the profit-margin ratio of the business? Is this business functioning at a 30 percent profit margin? Are fees set too low to generate sufficient income? Are expenses too high? What is the monthly overhead? Further investigation of other functions of the business could provide information about scheduling procedures and about collecting payments at the time of service versus allowing clients to be billed for sessions.

If the fictional business owner has all of this vital information to review and an understanding of what the numbers mean, it may be possible for him or her to do something to rectify the current negative owner's equity account. Numbers do tell the story, and clearly they're saying that help is needed.

18

SETTING A SCHEDULE: BUT FIRST, A SHORT STORY

The weekend was planned. Family members had put the dates on their calendars and had made the necessary travel arrangements. We would be coming from various points across the country to share a weekend of reconnection, fun, food, and lively conversation.

I arrived at my brother's home to find my niece sitting in front of her computer, looking distraught. She told me the rest of the clan had gone out on errands, but she had stayed to work on a project for her new job. After greetings and hugs, I raved about how great her amazingly toned body was—ten years of teaching yoga and Pilates looked mighty good on her. But I could see that something more was going on with her.

I asked about her new job, and her eyes began to well up with tears. She explained that she was in the process of trying to straighten out the "mess" she had created. She had mixed up some customer orders, sending the wrong information about deliveries on the wrong dates to the wrong customers. There were many aspects of the job that she felt confident about, but she feared her deficiencies in this area would stand in the way. She had to keep track of the many customers, their preferences, the money, and on and on—how could she keep all of that stuff straight?

I've been close to my niece since she was a baby, and while I knew this aspect of her job was not her strong suit, I knew too that she was more than capable of performing the functions. The key was to establish a system that would work for her. First, though, I had to reframe the problem in a way that removed the personal failure she felt and replace it with the concept of "the smart way to do business."

I explained to her that in my work, I get to know a lot about different people and that our topics of conversation involve more than just fights with spouses. I have worked with pilots for major airlines and have found that they're extremely intelligent. But even those exceptionally smart people, who have flown giant airplanes around the world hundreds of times, have a procedure that they must do every time before takeoff. It's called the "pilot's checklist." No responsible pilot would ever consider taking off without going through it and literally ticking off every item on the list as they check it. When I board an airplane, I am comforted by the fact that pilots follow the checklist.

My niece began to relax a bit. "Hmm, I could make a checklist for my work, and before I close an order, I could check off everything to be sure the order is exactly what the customer requested." She got it.

No longer burdened with a feeling of not being smart enough or worries that something was wrong with her brain, she quickly started setting up her own checklist. She then had a completely different attitude and a renewed confidence in herself and her ability to perform her job.

Setting a Schedule: But First, a Short Story

And so for you, my reader, I am creating a business checklist that is structured in a way that will not feel overwhelming. Its purpose is to serve as a guide—a reminder—of what you need to do and when. At the end of the list is a brief description of each item on it, and I have purposefully kept all information as succinct as possible.

If you would like, you can download a copy of this checklist from our website, www.savvymoneybooks.com. Keep it conveniently located so you can refer to it on a regular basis.

Business Checklist

Daily: Complete a daily sheet or enter daily information into your therapy software.
If you use a credit card machine, close out your day and confirm that the totals match.
Update money software account for payments made or money deposited.

Weekly: Run a cash-flow statement.

Monthly: Prepare income statement for that month.
Review monthly practice summary sheet.
Perform a bank reconciliation.
Review credit card statements.

Quarterly: Prepare quarterly income statement.
Calculate your profit-margin ratio.
Prepare balance sheet.
Pay retirement account contribution.
Review your savings accounts.
Pay estimated income taxes.

Annually: Prepare annual income statement.
Review annual practice summary statement.
Prepare annual cash flow.
Calculate your profit-margin ratio.
Prepare balance sheet.
Pay retirement account contribution.
Review savings accounts.
Prepare and file your tax return.
Plan for the next year.

Details and Explanations of Checklist Items

Daily

The **daily sheet** (see a copy of this sheet in the appendix or download a copy from our website) provides a place to list names, session codes, amounts charged, and money collected. Also list on the daily sheet any checks you receive from insurance companies or clients who mail in payments. If you are utilizing a therapist software program, use the daily activity page to compile this information.

Credit card payments are listed on the daily sheet. Confirm that the total dollar amount of credit card payments recorded on it is the same as the settlement statement you run off of your credit card machine. Not doing so can create problems later, as a situation that occurred at our office recently demonstrated. One of the therapists had a new assistant; unbeknownst to the therapist, she was running the credit card payments under my name instead of my colleague's. At the end of the day, I saw I had too much money in total credit card sales. I assumed someone would notice it and talk to me about it the next day. No one said a word. Two days later the same thing happened. Still, no one commented that they were coming up short on their daily credit card collections. I went to the therapist with the new assistant and asked if she was coming up short. She didn't know. She explained that she didn't track her collections or balance her daily charges. To rectify this, my colleague had to go through her calendar, files, and other records to find the credit card transaction slips that had my name instead of hers on them. She could have avoided all of that simply by confirming the amount of daily charges and daily collections at the end of the day.

Update your money software program with **bill payments** you have made plus **deposits** you have entered into your bank account. Get in the habit of checking your business bank account to confirm that all deposits are reflected properly in your account.

Weekly

Check **cash flow**, monies in and out, for the past week. Then look at the cash you need for the next week's expenses. Your money software will include a list of all of the expenses you'll need to pay and the dates on which you should pay them. I also keep a monthly Excel spreadsheet with expected payments due for each week. I have included a copy of this sheet on the website and in the appendix. Your software also does this for you. Check your cash balance, add the expenses you expect to pay in the next week, and verify that you have enough cash to cover upcoming expenses.

Review **savings accounts** on a regular basis. Your business savings account should preferably have six months' worth of overhead in it to cover an economic downturn or a personal issue that keeps you from working. Take into account that some of the money in your savings account is for quarterly estimated taxes unless you set up a separate tax savings account.

Monthly

Compare the **income statement** to those of the previous months for the current year as well as to that of the same month last year. Is there an increase in revenue? Are there any significant changes in expenses?

Be certain to look at the totals for each expense category. You can expect most accounts to be about the same amount every month. If anything appears to be out of the ordinary, look into the explanation. The draw account is one that can easily expand. If you're taking extra money out of the business, confirm that the business can afford it.

At the end of every month, my biller provides me with a copy of the **practice summary sheet**. This is a list of all current clients, amounts charged, payments received on accounts, adjustments made, previous balances, and current balances. By reviewing this summary sheet, you'll know which accounts have balances due and which accounts have a credit amount. Be sure to discuss with your clients how they want to handle credits on their accounts. Are they to be refunded or applied to future charges?

Do a **bank reconciliation** every month. You will easily find any errors that occurred in the last 30 days and will be able to correct them. Imagine how much work this would be if you had to search for an error in the past 60, 90, 120 days. Not fun!

Review every item on your **business credit card statement**. Confirm that each expense is yours and there are no fraudulent charges. Of course, the best policy is to pay the accounts in full, given the excessive rates of interest credit card companies charge. Also be sure to make the credit card payment on time. Late fees rob you of your hard-earned money.

Quarterly

Your **quarterly income statement** shows a three-month record of your income and expenses. Again, follow the monthly procedure of reviewing your numbers, confirming that income amounts and all expenses are correct. Evaluate where you can make changes if needed.

Check your **profit margin ratio** to see if you're above 30 percent. If this number is lower than your previous quarter's, find out why. Did overhead go up? Did session numbers decline?

Money software can easily prepare your **balance sheet**. Confirm that all necessary items are in the system correctly to ensure its accuracy. Is your owner's equity account increasing?

You can make contributions to your **retirement account** as frequently as you'd like. The amounts you're allowed to contribute to the account depend upon the type of retirement account you have. It's much easier to contribute less money on a regular basis than to try to come up with a large amount of money at the end of the year. Weekly or monthly contributions are best, but quarterly contributions are acceptable.

Pay **quarterly estimated taxes** by the fifteenth of the month for the previous quarter. (See chapter 15.) Payments are due on April 15, June 15, September 15, and January 15. Even if you can't pay the full amount due, pay something. It will make it easier to pay your final annual tax bill.

Annual

The **annual income statement** should be easy to run if you've been tracking the accounts every month all year. Once you have verified correct entry of all figures, you can run the income statement. Again, analyze it, compare it with past statements, and study it for possible alterations that could contribute to a greater income for the next year.

You'll also need to do your **annual cash flow statement** every year. How much cash did you put into the business, and how much did you take out of it? Remember that cash may or may not be income.

The **balance sheet** for the year ending will provide you with a list of your business's assets and liabilities and the owners' equity as of the date of the year's end, which is usually December 31. Compare this balance sheet with the previous year's year-end balance sheet. Is your business growing? Are the assets increasing and the liabilities decreasing?

The **annual practice summary sheet** will tell you exactly how much money you collected for services rendered during the year and is the amount that you will report as gross revenue on your tax return. This information is generated by a therapy software program; it tracks all of your clients' accounts, the amounts they owed, and the amounts they paid during the year. Be sure to print it out.

The **profit-margin ratio** for the entire year's work will tell you the percentage of the revenue collected that is yours. (See chapter 11.) View this number as a guide for the next year. What income strategies and expenses could you change to increase this number for the next year?

Annual **retirement account contributions** allowed are

based on the type of plan you have and the amount of net income you report on your tax return. Discuss with your tax preparer how much you're allowed to contribute for the tax year that just ended and when you're allowed to make your final contribution for that year.

Review your savings accounts at the end of each year. Did you make the goal you set for yourself for savings this past year? What is your goal for the next year? Sometime in January your bank will send you a 1099 to report the interest you earned on the savings account; put this 1099 form with the other tax papers for your tax preparer.

Your **tax-preparer accountant meeting** will be coming up soon. Prepare early rather than waiting until far into February or March to gather up the papers, statements, and other documents you'll need to take with you. Have a specific file or a large envelope in which to place these important papers. As soon as you have your financial data together, schedule your meeting with your tax preparer. Don't wait until April to do this. Your tax preparer will be very busy and possibly very grouchy if you delay.

Start **making plans for your business**. Don't wait until the end of December; start looking for ways to improve your services sooner than that. Have you developed more productive methods to enhance the work you do? Review your policies, procedures, paperwork, fee structure, payment options, and professional goals for you and your business. The knowledge and understanding of the financial data that you now have at your disposal will guide you in making adjustments that will increase revenue and allow you to work smarter, not harder.

As you go through this entire list, it probably will feel like a lot. But as you can see, these are the expected practices of any business person over the period of one year. Once the structure is in place, gathering and organizing the financial data will become second nature. Your office assistant or bookkeeper can enter the data and print out the necessary financial statements. If, on the other hand, your business is small, as long as you have good money software, you won't have to spend much time entering the data, printing out statements, and reviewing your financial status.

As you have probably figured out by now, I love the way these numbers come together. Each statement gathers information from another statement, each one painting a different section of the financial picture. Finally, the financial statements come together to reveal the entire picture. And now, with that before you, you can analyze the business, make decisions, and create plans to make your business even better.

You have now met and become friends with each one of the business numbers and financial statements necessary to manage a successful business. My hope for you is that as you implement these procedures into your business, you'll experience the financial serenity that comes with being a Money-Savvy Therapist.

About the Author

Alexa Elkington, MFT, is a psychotherapist in Las Vegas, Nevada and the co-owner of Summerlin Counseling Associates. While raising her five children, she worked as a tax accountant, with many medical practice clients. After realizing her dream to be a therapist, she naturally applied what she had learned about finances to her counseling practice. Only later did she discover that having a business mindset was a rarity in the field. This prompted her to write *Financial Savvy for Therapists* to help others master handling their money, and, in doing so, grow their business.

Appendix

DAILY SHEET

Date _____

Client Name	CPT Code	Dx	Fee	Adj	Cash	Check	Credit	Comments
			$	$	$	$	$	Total $ Recv'd:

Totals: Sessions: _____

CPT Codes

90791 Initial Interview
90832 Indiv Psychoth (16 - 37 min)
90834 Indiv Psychoth (38 - 52 min)
90837 Indiv Psychoth (53 min or longer)
90843 Family therapy w/o pt
90847 Family therapy w pt
90849 Multi family group Th
90853 Group Therapy
90857 Interact group therapy
90880 Medical Hypno
90887 Consult w family
90889 Prep of report, consultation, exec coaching

Appendix

Expense	Month Expenses due by Week for Cash Flow					
	Jan-16					
	Week 1	Week 2	Week 3	Week 4	Week 5	Totals
Savings						
Rent						
Auto Fuel						
Auto Loan						
Auto Insur						
Auto Maint						
Bank Fees						
Cell phones						
Dues						
Insur Health						
Insur Liab						
Insur Renter						
Interest						
Meals & Ent						
Prof Assist						
Prof Devel						
Retirement						
Supplies						
Taxes, local						
Taxes Fed						
Taxes State						
Travel Air						
Travel Auto Rental						
Travel Food						
Travel Hotel						
Travel other						
Utilities						
DRAW						
TOTAL						

CPSIA information can be obtained
at www.ICGtesting.com
Printed in the USA
FFOW03n1046140317
33410FF